ALL YOU NEED TO KNOW ABOUT PUBLIC RELATIONS

ALL YOU NEED TO KNOW ABOUT PUBLIC RELATIONS

An Entrant's Guide to the PR and Communications Industry

BY

ADRIAN WHEELER

emerald
PUBLISHING

United Kingdom – North America – Japan – India
Malaysia – China

Emerald Publishing Limited
Emerald Publishing, Floor 5, Northspring, 21-23 Wellington Street,
Leeds LS1 4DL.

First edition 2025

Reprints and permissions service
Contact: www.copyright.com

British Library Cataloguing in Publication Data
A catalogue record for this book is available from the British Library

ISBN: 978-1-83608-841-7 (Print)
ISBN: 978-1-83608-838-7 (Online)
ISBN: 978-1-83608-840-0 (Epub)

INVESTOR IN PEOPLE

This book is dedicated to Annie Wheeler

I didn't really know what PR was until I started working for a public relations company.

—*Brennan Drake,* Best Communications

We used to think PR was all about fashion and celebrities, but it's much more interesting than that.

—*Dara Nacheva,* RMS PR

A good PR story is infinitely more effective than a front-page ad … we put enormous weight on our PR people.

—*Sir Richard Branson,* Virgin Group

CONTENTS

PREFACE

I meet a lot of public relations people in my working life. Colleagues, clients, competitors and trainees.

We often get talking about how we started out in PR.

Very few of us set our sights on a PR career when we were at school, college or university.

Most of us say things like: 'I just stumbled into it' or 'an opportunity came up' or 'it just happened'.

At the same time, we all say we can't imagine doing anything else.

This made me wonder: how many people are there who'd be happy and successful in PR but just don't know enough about it when they're choosing their future career?

This book contains my own opinions plus advice and ideas from many other PR people who remember how hard it can be to find out what working in PR is like.

We all hope you'll find this book useful. We want thousands of people with different ideas, talents, backgrounds, attitudes, knowledge, experience, perspectives and convictions to come and work alongside us. *Diversity* really is the heart and soul of successful PR and communications.

We can make you a promise: if you set out on a career in PR, you'll never regret it.

ACKNOWLEDGEMENTS

The author would like to thank the following individuals, who have generously contributed their ideas, experience and advice to the production of this book: Mark Adams, Richard Bailey, Chloe Baker, Alexandra Bingham, Luke Blair, Ann-Marie Blake, Christopher Broadbent, Dominic Church, Brennan Drake, Steve Dunne, Euan Edworthy, Jackie Elliot, Itty Elora, Richard Fogg, Virginia Hawkins, Oli Higgs, Souha Khairallah, Stuart McBride, Trevor Morris, Steve Norris, Carsten Priebe, Jan Stannard, Ben Steele, Stephanie Umebuani, Thomas Wheeler and Lionel Zetter.

1

PR AND COMMUNICATIONS –
A GREAT CAREER CHOICE

If you're looking at this book, you've probably heard something about public relations (PR) and think it might be the right career for you.

If so, you are almost certainly right.

From small beginnings only 50 years ago, PR has grown like topsy. There are now nearly 100,000 of us just in the United Kingdom. This country's annual PR budget is estimated at £15 billion.

As an industry, PR and communications is still growing. We have big, global firms with thousands of employees; medium-sized firms covering several industry sectors, regions or countries; and smaller firms specialising in specific areas (like healthcare or financial services) or specific services (like Environmental, Social, Governance (ESG), social media, crisis management or internal communications). These days every company, charity, public sector organisation – and celebrity – has its own PR team.

A FAST-GROWING PROFESSIONAL SERVICES INDUSTRY

What is driving the growth of PR and communications? The simple answer is that it works.

We all need information and advice about what to do with our money and time. Which is the best car for someone like me? Where will our family get the best holiday within our budget? Do I want to live in Edinburgh – or Glasgow? Work for GSK – or Novartis? Support Greenpeace – or Friends of the Earth? Put savings into a pension now – or later? Buy an air fryer – or not?

Advertising used to be the only way for normal people to find out. But *you* never really believed advertising, and nor did anyone else.

Then came PR – journalists and other independent experts, first in print, on radio and on TV, then on digital platforms and social media. We trusted them then and we still do. We know that they are paid to get things right and tell us what we need to know in an entertaining way. The media hate getting things wrong and there are sub-editors, editors, legal departments and watchdogs to make sure they very rarely do.

PR AND THE MEDIA WORK HAND-IN-HAND

Where do the media get their information from? Much of what's published in the media today comes from PR agencies and PR departments. Us. That's one reason for PR's growth: the media demand news, stories, content, material – and PR people supply it.

Employers and clients care about 'ROI – return on investment'. The ROI of PR surpassed the ROI of traditional advertising 20 years ago. That's another reason for PR's growth: it often performs the same function as advertising (sales) but it works much better and it costs much less.

PERSUASIVE COMMUNICATION

But what exactly is PR?

Ask 10 different PR people and you'll get 10 different definitions (I've done this). Some people call it 'a mixture of art and science'. Others think of it as 'a combination of maths and magic'. But there's a common thread: PR is a form of *persuasive communication*, often – though not always – with the aim of selling products, brands and services in competitive marketplaces.

Working in PR lets you get a deep understanding of various different industries and other areas of human activity. You learn a lot about a lot. As a career, it offers amazing opportunities – including the chance of working in other countries. It stands out because there really is plenty of 'fun stuff' – but there's also a good deal of sheer hard work.

Ann-Marie Blake is a well-known consultant,
advisor and trainer in communications

THIRD PARTIES GIVE CREDIBILITY

PR usually works – though not always – through 'third parties'. Reporters, journalists, broadcasters, editors and presenters are good examples of third parties whose independent judgement and experience make us all pay attention to what they say.

But a trusted third party could also be a university professor who's written books and appears on TV ... or an influencer whose channel attracts half a million followers ... or it could be Eva on the fourth floor, who knows everything there is to know about gardening ... or childcare ... or luxury cruises ... or trainers.

Trainers – that's a good example. Was there a sports star at college who always had the latest from Nike (or Adidas, or Puma or Reebok)? We may have watched his or her performance with admiration and bought the same brand of trainers. Did we know that he or she was a 'Brand Ambassador' for Nike?

PR was the first job I ever had. I love everything about helping organisations tell their story: the planning, the writing, the creativity, the engagement, the reporting ... Everything. Fantastic.

Mark Adams co-founded Text 100, the world's
biggest tech PR firm (now Next 15)

PR CHANGES PEOPLE'S BEHAVIOUR

Trying to pin down what PR is and isn't can get boring. We hope you'll get a fuller picture as you look through this book. One more common factor before we get going: PR is always about *changing people's behaviour* – choosing this new restaurant rather than the one we've always gone to for special occasions ... switching to Samsung from Apple after five years ... deciding on Sardinia rather than Tenerife ... buying a flat in Greenwich after living north of the river since we were born...

How does this happen? Isn't it all about receiving information which attracts our interest, arouses our curiosity, makes us think and then provokes us to change our minds?

How does that work? Isn't it mostly about creativity – ideas that surprise us, catch our attention, amuse us or entertain us, draw us in, satisfy our curiosity and make us wonder?

We'll be hearing more about *creativity* as we go through the book. For now, let's just say that it's the key talent for successful PR people.

Here's the good news: *we are all creative*. Psychologists and neuroscientists can prove it, even though some of us *know* we're creative and others don't think they are. But creativity isn't the whole story. In the next chapter, we'll think about why some people are well-suited to a career in PR and others less so.

A GREAT CAREER CHOICE

There are other reasons why PR and communications is a great career choice. Yes, I admit I am biassed, and so are the other people whose advice is quoted in this book. But we are also right.

You can advance very rapidly – you don't have to wait years to get promoted.

You can earn good money while you are still young enough to enjoy it.

You can set up your own PR firm and become wealthy. In some cases, seriously wealthy.

You can learn a lot about something that interests you (in fact, you'll have to).

You can learn a lot about what's going on in the world (again, you'll have to).

You can become a close and trusted advisor to your clients or employer.

You can see the work you do making a difference before your very eyes.

You will have more sheer fun than anyone you know in other professions.

PR is one of the most exciting career choices. You work with senior people at a young age. If you enjoy fun, pressure and a bit of chaos from time to time, you'll feel at home in PR. There are literally no two days the same. It's a broad church, there are no barriers to entry, so there's a place for almost everyone – the industry is big and growing, and is hungry for diverse talents. If you like routine, PR might not be the best choice for you ... but if you enjoy challenges, learning and finding out about new things, there is simply no better career.

Rich Fogg, CEO of CCGroup

IS PR THE RIGHT CHOICE FOR EVERYONE?

But is PR *really* heaven on earth? *I* think so, and so do most of my friends, but we must be realistic. As you will discover in the following pages, PR is the *perfect* career for some people, a *great* career for a lot of people and the *wrong* career for other people. For instance:

It's not a profession, it's a business. The correct definition is 'professional business service'. No-one *has* to hire a PR firm or a PR person – people only pay us because they think we will deliver the results they are hoping for.

It's an insecure career. If your client or your employer decides they're not getting what they hoped for, that's it. At least, in that particular job or that particular agency. PR is also full of opportunities to move on somewhere else. Most PR people (though not all) have had two or three jobs by the time they are 30.

PR PEOPLE AND JOURNALISTS ARE
SIMILAR IN MANY WAYS

As it happens, PR people are – in this way – on the same wavelength as their media customers. *If you want to know more about the life and work of journalists, there is no better guide than* 'My Trade' *by Andrew Marr.*

Most people in PR work long hours. We are always trying to please, surprise and delight our clients or employers. We always feel that we need to prove our worth – we feel we are only as good as what we delivered yesterday, last week and last month. Here again, we resemble people working in the media.

Obviously that's not the full picture … relationships, reputations and track-records matter … though if you want a safe and solid career with a gold-plated pension at the end of it, you might want to think about something else.

But if you love enjoy tension and excitement … not really knowing what comes next … feeling confident but *not certain* that things will work out well … if you can deal with a certain amount of stress and come up smiling … then PR could be just the thing for you. If you are good at 'keeping a lot of balls in the air' and get a buzz from unexpected challenges, the world of PR – where no two days are ever the same – could be exactly the right career.

The great thing about PR is the variety, the different types of projects and sectors you work in, the interesting people you meet, the freedom and creativity you have, and the appreciation you can receive for your skills. Another is the fact that you can start out either with an agency or with an in-house department – and switch later on. Each have their plus and minus factors, so it's mainly a question of personal preference. But you have the choice. I'd have to agree with the author that PR is the best career in the world – but, of course, it's not for everyone.

Luke Blair, Director of Communications at an NHS hospital group

THE PUBLIC IMAGE OF PR

As a professional business service, PR doesn't have the reputation it deserves. We are 'cobbler's children'. If you are thinking about PR as a career, you may be slightly concerned by the way some people talk about PR – particularly journalists (it's a love–hate relationship).

A lot of ink and electrons have been wasted by people trying to portray PR as a dark art. The term 'spin doctor' may be familiar to you. But the Peter Mandelsons and Lord Bells are very rare and are usually found in political PR – *public affairs*. There is something not-quite-right about high-profile PR people: it's our clients who are meant to be famous, not us.

You may have seen or heard about 'Absolutely Fabulous' (*Ab Fab*), a BBC hit comedy in the 1990s. Jennifer Saunders' character was said to be based on Lynne Franks, a very successful PR person specialising in fashion and celebrities, with an outsize personality. Saunders and Joanna Lumley, her co-star, were so funny that their caricature of PR made a lasting impact. But it was a comedy.

Lynne Franks is a rare example of a PR person who became well-known outside the PR community. There are a few others – Mark Borkowski, for instance, who is a true creative genius and a much-quoted public figure – but there aren't many. This is, I think, as it should be: when PR people become the story, something has gone wrong.

So if you really want to be famous (rather than rich or happy), PR might not be for you.

Students' Impressions of the PR Industry

We asked six people on humanities and business studies courses for their impressions of PR and if they thought of PR as a possible career.

Fiona: *PR is controlling how the public views a product or a person. Yes, PR could be a career choice for me – all my internships have been involved in marketing, which is close.*

Tomas: *If you take football as an example, PR means popularity – whether or not the player is on good form. Some footballers have terrific PR, no matter what happens on the pitch. For myself, I think it's important to know how PR works, whatever you do – but it's probably not ideally suited to my personal skills.*

Mai: *PR is the art of disseminating information about products and people – changing public opinion. Yes, PR could be a career path for me – but only if it's for musicians or artists, because that's the area where I want to spend my working life.*

Peter: *PR is about impacting how something or someone is seen by the general public. It's not an option I have seriously considered as a career: I've had internships in marketing, but my personal goal is to work in the film industry.*

Louna: *It's being able to change the way something is viewed. Yes, it could be right for me, but at the moment I am very interested in learning how advertising works, so that's where I hope to start my career.*

Philip: *If you work in a PR agency you have to make sure your client is happy about their image. I wouldn't consider PR as a career, but I will definitely need to use PR in what I plan to do, which is music and fashion.*

EARLY ORIGINS IN THE UNITED STATES

The origins of modern PR go way back to the early 1900s in the United States. There are two recognised 'godfathers' of our industry. Ivy Lee was an author and public figure who – 100 years ago – advocated interaction, or *a conversation*, between organisations and members of the public. He called it 'the two-way street'. The word 'conversation' is now part of our daily vocabulary in PR and communications, but it was not until the widespread adoption of the internet (let's say around 2000) that interaction, or *engagement*, became a necessity rather than an option.

The other godfather, Ed Bernays, was an academic with numerous books and treatises to his credit. He was an expert in mass psychology, and was in fact a nephew of Sigmund Freud. Like Ivy Lee, he was hired by large US corporations to help manage their reputations, and ended up advising some of the biggest blue-chips as well as US government departments.

Our industry (craft, trade, business, discipline, occupation and line of work) has its roots in the East Coast universities – academic foundations of a high order. This book is not the place for a detailed history of global PR (if you want that, look in Appendix 1).

It's worth stating here and now that PR is a complicated professional business service, based on *both* scientific analysis and creative communications ability. It has proved its worth in the take-no-prisoners conditions of the free market: no-one has to hire a PR firm, and no-one does unless they want to. PR is in this way *unlike* accountancy, legal services or architecture, but *similar to* management consultancy, advertising and Harvard Business School.

What I love about this industry is how no two days will ever be the same. There is always something exciting around the corner. The work is highly rewarding. It also means staying organized, level-headed and calm under pressure and tight deadlines. The agency environment exposes you to a wide variety of clients, industries, journalists and colleagues with different skill-sets. This can help progress your career and knowledge very quickly. It's a dynamic industry. Creativity is at a premium. You need a natural ability to build and nurture relationships. If so, this is the career for you.

Virginia Hawkins, PR Consultant at Screaming Frog

PR is a very broad church. If you think you'd like to work in it, the first thing to consider is *who* you'd like to work for (or on behalf of) and *what* you'd like to do for them. If you work in PR you are always representing someone else – a brand, an industry, a cause, a product, a point of view ... like a lawyer, but much more interesting. Go online and explore. What appeals to you most? Internal communications, which is closely linked to HR? Public affairs, which is all about communicating with government and regulatory bodies? Media relations, which means forming close bonds with journalists? Digital? Knowing what aspect of PR feels best-aligned with your current interests and abilities will make it much easier to decide how to take that first step.

Stuart McBride is head of PR for a financial
trade association

In my experience, PR is a career ideally suited to people who are naturally curious, enjoy variety, have a genuine interest in current affairs, like storytelling and are good at building relationships with other people. There's a lot of strategic thinking involved – you need to be able to write compelling content – but before that you also need to be able to decide if this is the right thing for your organization to be saying, and why.

No two days are the same. One day you might be securing a media interview, the next you might be hit with a potential crisis, the next you could be working with colleagues to figure out how to win pole position in the media on a key issue. It isn't easy. You can work for weeks and nothing happens. You have to be resilient.

I love my work. It's challenging, stretching and I'm gaining new knowledge and new skills every week. At the same time, it's demanding – you have to stay ahead of the game, all the time, because the competition for attention is tough. It suits me, and I think it would suit everyone who's a good communicator and likes a bit of a battle.

Alexandra Bingham, Senior Media and
Communications Officer at Mercy Corps

What Does 'Storytelling' Mean?

We hear this word a lot in PR and communications. We might imagine that it's a special ability which can be studied, examined, analysed, written about and learned at university.

It's not. All it means is being interesting when we talk or write.

Imagine we are in the pub or wine-bar with our friends. There's always someone, isn't there, who captures the attention of the group … they've got the 'gift of the gab', or they 'just know how to tell a good story'. Everyone listens, everyone laughs.

What are they doing? It's not magic. They are telling us things we want to know, they are not wasting our time, they are keeping us on the edge of our seats, they are making us want to know more, they are making the whole experience enjoyable, and they are leaving us with something we want to remember, and maybe want to share with other people.

That's PR!

You Ought to Know About Behavioural Economics

In the last 20 years, scientists have used MRI, PET scans and similar techniques to figure out how and why people pay attention to certain things (and not others) and why they remember certain things (and not others). As a result, they buy some things and not others.

This is obviously key to successful persuasive communications. Long story short, it turns out that emotional engagement is much more important than rational explanation.

Watch lectures, talks and presentations by Rory Sutherland of Ogilvy on YouTube.

If you are intrigued and fascinated by what Roy Sutherland and others like him say, you will probably enjoy a career in PR. If not, probably not.

This could be a good 'acid test' as to whether or not PR is for you.

MY OWN STORY

I worked as a mechanic, swimming-pool attendant and sign-writer before I got a break in local newspapers as a trainee reporter. I learnt the basics of putting a story together so an editor would accept it (rather than throw it at my head, as mine often did).

I went to work at Watergate Bay in Cornwall. There I learnt how local media, TV and radio were avid for stories with a local angle. Also that if a story looked big enough, the national media would take it. You just had to ring up and tell them about it.

That was all it took to get me into PR and learn the ropes. I started my own agency with a couple of friends. We were very lucky – great clients, great colleagues. Later I worked for Grey Advertising, setting up PR offices for them all over EMEA.

If you have read this far, you know that I have a passion for PR and everything about it. Most of my friends are either PR people or journalists. I love what I do, who I do it for and who I do it with.

I'm not an objective witness. But I don't think I can be. PR is the best career in the world – for very many people – and I want to encourage you to go for it.

Unless you decide you shouldn't.

2

ARE YOU RIGHT FOR PR? IS PR RIGHT FOR YOU?

As Rich Fogg says, public relations is a broad church. It's possible for almost anyone to find their niche in PR and communications. I've mentioned that diversity – *every kind of diversity* – is at the heart of successful PR agencies and departments; one of the great pleasures of my own career has been working with other people of every imaginable type.

But this doesn't really help you if you're wondering whether to start your career in PR or – for example – travel. So in this chapter, we'll try to narrow down the factors that may be a bit more useful if you're trying to make that decision.

APTITUDES

You Need to Enjoy Writing and Reading

PR people spend half their working lives writing media material of one kind or another – press releases, news features, thought-leadership pieces, case studies, briefing papers, blog-posts, (the list goes on) and a lot of time reading things – media coverage, research, market analyses, surveys and so on.

If you enjoy writing and reading, you can expect to like PR work.

You are probably an avid consumer of news, current affairs and opinion media already. If you're a humanities student, you most likely read a lot of books and enjoy it. You probably take an interest in other forms of media too – TV, perhaps, radio, podcasts, etc. – and you'll have your preferred social media channels. You may even devote time to attending talks and conferences about subjects that interest you.

Key Interview Question

Employers often ask would-be PR recruits: 'Which are your favourite sources of news?' If the person says: 'I don't know, really' or 'None'... that's more-or-less the end of the interview. This does happen from time to time.

Another question is: 'What books are you reading at the moment?' If the answer is 'None' this won't necessarily disqualify the candidate but it's not a positive sign. Having a natural interest in the news and the media, and having an aptitude for learning things through reading books, are both characteristics of someone who, other things being equal, is cut out for a career in PR and communications.

You Need to Be Curious About What's Going On

Successful PR people usually know *a lot* about several things and *something* about almost everything. This is because there's virtually nothing in the world of human affairs that *definitely won't* have an effect on the brands or companies they are looking after. Any kind of change could be important – it could mean an opportunity, it could pose a problem. PR people need good antennae.

This means spending a fair amount of time keeping up with the news – what's going on in the world, what's going on in the United Kingdom and what's going on in a particular industry. No-one can do this without having a good deal of natural curiosity, and this doesn't start when you join a PR team – you already have it, and probably always have had.

This is something PR people share with journalists. *They* always want to know who, what, where, when, why and how. So do we.

Successful PR people use what they learn through *curiosity* to work out where and how their clients can take advantage of trends. Or the opposite. This means that reading and listening to the news *every day* is super-important – a basic PR habit. If you don't already watch, hear, read or browse the news on a daily basis – or want to – PR, *which is all about the news and what's new*, may not be the best choice of career.

Some PR people become 'news junkies' – checking out the media round-the-clock.

You Need to Be Interested in Human Behaviour

PR people are paid to be *persuasive communicators*. This means knowing why different kinds of people think certain things, feel certain things and behave in certain ways. If you don't understand them, you can't communicate with them effectively. Obviously, you'll only be able to understand them if you're interested in them.

This doesn't mean you have to be a psychologist (though there are a number of trained psychologists working in PR and communications). It just means you take more interest in other people than, probably, your friends do. You may even have a personal interest in psychology and be learning about it in your spare time.

Some PR people have a gift which can be called *insight*. They just know, intuitively, how others are feeling and what will make them change how they feel, think and act. Some PR people (like me) don't have this gift; we have to do it the hard way. In either case, possessing a natural interest in the how's and why's of human behaviour is a good sign that you will probably be happy and successful in PR.

PR people should enjoy reading. We are storytellers. Reading different kinds of material helps us tell stories better. A PR person also needs to be a 'people person'. We must be interested in other people and their stories. This means curiosity ... enjoying digging and finding out more ....

Ben Steele, Communications Officer at Sightsavers

You need to be naturally curious, enjoy variety and have a genuine interest in current affairs. You need to be good at storytelling and relationship-building. You should also be adaptable and able to think on your feet.

Alexandra Bingham, Senior Media and Communications Officer at Mercy Corps

PERSONALITY AND OUTLOOK

It Helps to Be Sociable and Enjoy the Company of Others

There's a popular image of PR people as 'the life and soul of the party'. Some are, but not all. You don't need to be an extrovert – at the same time, it's not a good career for introverts.

Most PR people have an outgoing personality. They really like meeting new people, listening to people, asking questions and learning from others. They also like sharing their own ideas and opinions (don't we all?) but, on balance, they do more listening than speaking.

They usually have a lot of friends and spend more time in company than alone. Usually, but not always: if a PR person is working on developing their 'personal brand' they may spend more evenings on their laptop than socialising with colleagues, friends and contacts.

Most successful PR people develop strong views – whether they work in an agency or in-house, they are there to give specialist advice. It is not a career for 'shrinking violets' – though most of us will refrain from saying too much in the early stages of our careers.

You Probably Like Knowing Things First and Making Recommendations

Are you the kind of person who gets a kick out of knowing the best new restaurant, a great new offer from a holiday company, which new release to stream, the best new treats for dogs, the smart way to jump the queue for festival tickets ...? Do people come to you for advice on gardening… fashion… movies… recipes… exercise… diets… anything? If so, you are probably a natural-born PR person.

We make our living as *persuasive communicators*. If you do this anyway, just for fun, you will almost certainly like doing the same thing, for clients, for money.

This might sound like an over-simplification, but I don't think so. PR people provide a wide range of communications services to their employers or clients – we'll give some brief descriptions later in the book – but most clients or employers, most of the time, want their PR people to help them sell more of their product or brand to more people, in more places, more often, more efficiently, so that their company makes more money.

It doesn't have to be commercial. Maybe you are an ardent advocate for a good cause like sustainability, fairness, justice, support for people who are less-privileged, animal welfare, political freedom and human rights, etc. If so – if you are voluntarily working to persuade people that their ideas and behaviour should change in some way – you are very likely a natural PR or public affairs person, and this could be the right career for you.

You Should Have a Positive, Optimistic Outlook

Do you need to be full of the joys of Spring 24 hours a day? No. You are not Julie Andrews. Do you need to have a generally sunny, up-beat, can-do approach to life? Yes, very much so.

They say that human beings are either radiators or drains. Radiators make people smile when they come into a room. Drains … don't. Radiators get listened to and are good at persuading people to think and feel differently. Drains … don't. We all want to be surrounded by radiators and we tend to avoid the company of drains.

The difference, of course, is positivity.

Some people are born radiators, but even if we're not, we can cultivate radiator behaviour. When you're deciding about your future career, ask yourself the question: 'Am I a natural radiator? Do I brighten up the atmosphere and make people around me feel better? If not, could I do that if I really wanted to?'

Great *persuasive communications* – whether face-to-face, in writing, on-screen, through headphones or whatever – has a lot to do with putting a smile on people's faces. We all know that from our own experience. If we can do it – or learn to do it – we will be successful in PR.

It Helps to Be Ambitious in Any Career – But Specially in PR and Communications

PR and communications is highly competitive. If you've read this far, you already know that the industry is large and growing, with lots of opportunities. But it isn't a walk in the park.

PR is creative, sociable and enjoyable. There are no barriers to entry or rapid promotion. This makes the industry attractive to talented people who – for whatever reason – decide *not* to go into investment banking, accountancy, law or management consulting, etc.

When we work in PR, we are competing against talented people who *could* have pursued a traditional career if they had wanted to. I am not just saying this: at my agency there was one young woman who could easily have been a university professor by 30. She just didn't want to. As things turned out, she was a director at 24. Another recruit joined us from Vilnius (also a young woman). She had a master's degree in quantum mechanics. She said: 'I didn't want to stand in front of a blackboard for the rest of my life'. She switched to PR, was very successful, and never regretted her change of direction.

She told us she liked PR because it was a kind of 'cat' profession. 'It works if you can't see it working, but as soon as you see it working it stops working'.

Rupert came to our agency from a fast-track career in the city. He was doing very well but then thought: 'No ... I want to do something more creative in my career'. When he told his mother about this decision she asked only one question: 'Rupert ... will you wear a suit?'

I hope the point is clear: PR welcomes a whole variety of backgrounds and talents, which includes people who are super-able and very ambitious. You can have a *good* career in PR if you are not particularly ambitious, but a *fabulous* career if you are. Most employers will look for signs of ambition at your interviews.

When I was a young agency person a client's CEO told me: `Only ever hire people who are better than you in some way'. It was the best business advice I ever heard.

Jackie Elliot, CEO of one of London's most successful PR agencies, told me her recruitment policy. 'I asked them where they wanted to end up. If they said "I want your job" I was quite likely to hire them on the spot'.

WORKING STYLE

If you're at university or college, you might not yet know what your preferred style is. But let's just say a couple of things about the kind of working habits which are connected with success in PR.

Team Player or Solo Artiste?

Half the time in a PR agency or department you will work as a member of a team. Not always, but even when you're working alone the product of your work will usually be combined with that of your colleagues, changed by their opinions and in any case presented to the client or senior person as the creation of the group you belong to.

Not always, of course, but mostly, it's the nature of PR work to be *produced* in teams, *presented* for approval in teams and *executed* by teams once it's been given the 'green light'.

The other half of the time you work on your own – but mostly in order to prepare a contribution to the collective work of the team – which might be a permanent, solid group that you are a member of, or might be a temporary collaboration, or could be a group of people you have never met because they live in Paris, San Francisco, Orlando and Bogota.

Unlike journalism, PR is structured in a way that suits team players better than solo artistes. You are a member of the choir, not a diva. This is, of course, no different from how most other creative industries work, and the universal adoption of online collaborative tools makes teamwork even easier, whether we're separated by thousands of miles or just working from home.

> The kind of person who does well in PR is a people-person, energized by relationships and curious about what makes people tick. Someone who takes a keen interest in the world around them, in current affairs, reading and writing. Someone who is active in events – cultural, sporting, whatever. Someone who likes a busy life.
>
> *Luke Blair, Director of Communications at an NHS hospital group*

If you like routine, PR is probably not the career for you. The number one criterion is a command of the English language. Second is curiosity. You *must* be curious, wanting to know. You must be a *reader* – that can take various forms these days: many people take in the information they need while doing something else, like running. You *must* feel the need to keep up-to-date, 'ahead of the game', this means you always have something new to discuss with your client or employer. If you work in PR, you have to enjoy social interaction, be socially confident and possess what Rich Fogg calls 'social dexterity'. It's a kind of confidence that some people seem to have naturally and others can learn if they want to.

> PR is the most exciting thing you can do in an office. I really mean that. I can't think of a better career for people who like interesting challenges and can handle the pressure which is part and parcel of PR … no two days are the same and we never really know what to expect next.
>
> *Rich Fogg, CEO of CCGroup*

Personal Working Style

If you are at university or college, the pace and timing of your work is probably dictated by the term schedule or what your tutors ask you to deliver. But you may already have decided what kind of working routine suits you best.

First: predictability. Some people like to know that tomorrow will be much the same as today – no surprises. Fair enough – but people who prefer predictability probably won't be very happy working in PR.

Part of PR is *proactive* ('We've had a great idea! Let's do it!').

But a lot of PR is *reactive* ('Oh no! The government has just changed the law on diesel engines!' 'BetterBix have just launched a cereal with half the calories of our client's!' 'There's a political problem that means no-one can go to Mauritius anymore!').

We need to be resilient, cool, calm, collected (and, I would add, creative) when things happen that could harm, impinge on, jeopardise or threaten the business activities of our client or employer.

Is this you? Do you feel you can deal with events that no-one ever anticipated? Are you the kind of person who can spot opportunities and grab them before anyone else? Do you enjoy living, to some extent, 'on the edge'?

There is nothing wrong with routine. It may even make the world go round. But it's just not a feature of working in PR. Instead, we have surprises, shocks – maybe a bit of chaos, panic. Just like a media newsroom. If that sounds like fun, PR could be the right choice for you.

Nine to five? Rarely in PR and communications. We have to be available when our clients and the media need us, and that doesn't usually fit into a traditional working day. Most employers take great care that their people are never over-stressed, but it must be said that PR can make demands on your personal time that other careers don't.

Linked to this is 'the need for speed'. PR people often have to rush to meet a deadline. Sometimes two deadlines at once, or even three. This is mainly because of the frenetic pace at which the news media source, process and distribute stories, or 'content'. Not all PR work is about supplying the media, but a lot of it is, and working successfully with the media is still one of the most important requirements from clients and employers.

If you feel happy working under pressure – or think you will once you start work – the speed and pace of PR life will probably be exciting for you. There is, as the saying goes, 'never a dull moment'. But it doesn't suit everyone.

Someone who wants a quiet life, keeps themselves to them-selves and generally steers clear of crowds ... someone who likes to 'go by the book' and prefers clear rules ... someone who is self-contained and happiest working alone ... should probably think twice before considering a career in PR. PR isn't ideal, either, if you are a worrier and don't like risks. I often think of PR people as the ones at the front of the shop, happily serving customers and chatting away, while non-PR people are more likely to be in the store-room at the back, not talking to anyone much and buried in their everyday work.

Luke Blair, Director of Communications at an NHS hospital group

Don't overthink it. There are so many skills and qualities needed for a role in PR. Taking an interest in current affairs, an ability to research and analyse things critically, under-standing how people engage and communicate with each other in today's digital age ... it's all useful. Your background doesn't matter – your skills and experience are relevant, but most important of all is your interest in human beings and how to communicate with them.

Itty Elora, Talent Manager (PR, Comms and Advertising) at the Advertising Association

WHAT MAKES YOU HAPPY?

We'll talk about the financial rewards of a PR career later. Here we want to mention some of the *non-material* satisfactions of working in PR. You already know that it's a career unlike any other, and you know that people working in PR love what they do. The question is: does it match what you think *you* want from your working life?

Do you like helping other people?

PR and communications is a 'service business'. Every single thing we do, day in, day out, is for the benefit of someone else – our clients, in an agency or our employers if we work in an in-house PR team. If you get a lot of personal fulfilment out of helping other people solve problems and achieve success, you could be a natural fit for the PR industry.

You may be thinking that *all* professions are about helping other people. True, but there's a difference. You can't run a company without an accountant and you can't go to court unless you have a solicitor, and maybe also a barrister, representing you. By law. You *can* build a house without retaining an architect, but no-one in their right mind would do so. This is what a profession means: you are obliged to hire one if you need to get something done.

But *no-one* needs to hire a PR agency or employ a PR person. It's a completely voluntary choice. We are judged and paid *entirely* by how helpful our clients and employers think we are. How do they judge that? There are Key Performance Indicators (KPIs) and metrics galore, but most people, most of the time, evaluate the quality of their PR people by *how helpful* they seem to be.

PR and communications is a *true* service business. Not a profession, though it goes without saying that we behave professionally. If you are the kind of person who gets a buzz at the end of the day from knowing they've helped someone else get closer to their goals, PR could be just what you're looking for.

Do you like sharing in the success of your team?

Or are you someone who needs to score the winning goal to feel happy? There are not so many starring roles in PR and communications. If you are the kind of person who wants to stand out from the crowd – which is fine – PR might not be the best career choice for you. But if you get a thrill from playing a part, even a small part, in communal success – this is a career that you will like, and that will like you.

Do you like solving puzzles?

We don't mean crosswords. Most PR briefs (jargon for *instructions* from our client or employer) set out a *problem* they want us to help them solve. It could be expressed negatively: 'WOOFS are getting twice the coverage of WAGS – how can you change that?' or it could be expressed positively: 'An A-list celebrity has been taped giving her Labrador WAGS – how can we capitalise on that?'

Either way, it's an imaginative challenge. There are a hundred different steps that WAGS could take to achieve a bigger, better profile than WOOFS – leading to higher sales, which is our client's priority. We can't use the celebrity's name as an endorsement without her permission. Can we get it? If not, what else can we do? Most PR work is like this – the best answer is hardly ever obvious.

Do you think that coming up with creative, imaginative solutions to this kind of problem – in a team – would send you home at the end of the day feeling pleased with yourself?

Here's another one. You've been warned that an important journalist is about to write a piece demolishing your client's reputation as an honest businesswoman. You happen to know that he's been given a dossier of false facts by one of her competitors. You've got only 10 hours to stop him in his tracks. What will you do? How?

If this kind of knotty problem gets your pulse racing (and you don't mind staying online until 10.30 p.m. if need be) PR could be the career of your dreams. This kind of major opportunity or problem doesn't come up every day, of course, but you might be surprised how often they *do* land in the laps of the PR team.

Again, if this sounds like something you'd enjoy, PR could be very personally rewarding. If your feeling on reading these fictional examples is 'No thanks!' you should probably think about a career where the element of surprise and challenge is less prominent.

By the way, a lot of PR people *do* like crosswords and word-puzzles. By now, you can probably see why.

This problem-solving facility is often described as *creativity*. Some people are convinced that they're *not* creative, but this is wrong. Alan Arkin (actor, writer, director, musician and Oscar-winner) tells us in his autobiography 'An Improvised Life' that we are *all* creative – if you're a human being, it's in your DNA.

Why Creativity Matters in PR and Communications

Every adult in the United Kingdom receives 4,000 commercial messages through their eyes and ears every single day. We blot most of them out. No-one can absorb such a deluge.

At the same time, we have less patience than we used to. It's estimated that we only spend an average of 10 seconds consuming typical online news items (less than a goldfish, whose attention span is 14 seconds).

For persuasive communicators, this means that catching and holding the attention of our target audiences for more than 10 seconds is a challenge that's getting tougher all the time.

How do we handle it? The answer is creativity. We use words and images to present our messages in ways that seem original, different, fresh and attractive. If we're successful, our readers/viewers/listeners/browsers want to know more.

This is often called 'cut-through'.

Our goal is to be one of the few messages they take in and remember – not one of the thousands that get ignored.

Everyone has the ability to be creative, but some of us don't know it. Steve Jobs – one of the greatest creative geniuses of the 20th century – said that creative people don't actually do anything special ... they just see things that can be combined in new ways.

Anthony Brandt wrote a terrific book about human evolution (The Runaway Species) where he describes creativity as 'bending, breaking and blending'.

Biz Stone, Co-founder of the original Twitter, tells us that creativity is a renewable resource. 'You can never run out of ideas'.

There are techniques which PR and communications people use to generate creative ideas, either working on their own or in a team. People in PR quickly discover that they have creative talents which they may never have thought they possessed.

If you are thinking about a PR and communications career, you are probably interested in creativity. What makes a PR idea stand out from the crowd? You could check out 'Famous Campaigns', an excellent blog about great ideas in PR and marketing (famouscampaigns.com). You could also explore the award schemes run by the Public Relations and Communications Association (PRCA), the Chartered Institute of Public Relations and PR Week, the industry's own news-source. Or you could just enter 'creativity in PR' in your favourite search box and see what comes up (a lot).

Creativity is an important skill to possess. You'll need to find new, unique and engaging angles to make the headlines. The field is highly competitive with only a limited number of journalists who, for the most part, have seen it all before.

Virginia Hawkins, PR Consultant at Screaming Frog

Is PR and Communications ALL About New Ideas?

New ideas are super-important, but they're not the whole story. Successful PR people display many other skills, some of them vital and some of them handy but not essential.

We've talked a lot about writing already. It's the key skill, in my view (though other people wouldn't necessarily agree with me). If you work in PR and communications, you not only need to enjoy writing, you also have to be able to do it well. What does that mean?

Brevity is the key. Remember how short our attention spans are? No-one is going to plough through lengthy, shapeless prose in this day and age. PR writing is not like the kind of writing which gets us good marks at school and college. It's much more like media writing – or the kind of short, sharp messaging that advertising copywriters do well.

You might be good at this already, but few of us are. Organisations like the PRCA offer training courses in this kind of writing – for most of us, and for journalists and copywriters, it's a learned behaviour.

There's another key factor shared by all successful PR and communications people, but I'm not sure what the word is. It could be 'comprehension', or it could be 'analytical ability'. It means taking on board a lot of information, quickly, and combining it with what you already know to come up with a communications plan that stands a chance of capturing the audience's attention and changing their feelings, opinions and behaviour.

Successful PR people are sometimes described as possessing 'forensic skills' or being 'a quick study'. If you have the kind

> *of mind that can assemble a mass of data, pick out what matters and produce a plan that concentrates on the really important factors while discarding the rest ... you will be a success in PR and communications. To be candid, you will be a success in any other profession, but why should I tell you that in a book like this?*

Do you get a thrill out of seeing your writing published?

This could seem like a minor factor, but I don't think it is. We already know that being a keen reader and writer is one of the most important elements in becoming a successful PR person. At this stage – if you are still a student, or at school – you might not have done much writing for publication. But perhaps you have. And perhaps you get a lot of satisfaction, or pleasure, from seeing your words 'in print'.

After all, this is what inspires the thousands of authors and online hosts whose work *very occasionally* makes money, but usually doesn't.

When you work in PR and communications as a profession, your own name will hardly ever appear – if ever. But if you get a buzz when you see your writing published on behalf of your client – with her name, or maybe a journalist's name, as the byline – and this means something to you – it's a sign that a career in PR could be gratifying to you in a way that is beyond considerations of financial reward or personal credit.

Imagine being a playwright or scriptwriter for a hit show. The actors will be famous. The director might be. They get the spotlight. You don't – how many screenwriters do you know yourself? Probably one or two – or maybe none at all.

If you don't care very much about seeing your name in lights, but are quietly pleased when your work gets published – PR could be a great career for you as a writer.

Do you feel the need to have an effect on the world around you?

Some PR campaigns change the world. A good example is the 'Missing Letters' campaign encouraging people to donate blood. But these are few and far between. If you want to see more, check out the Famous Campaigns site (famouscampaigns.com).

Unlike advertising, most PR works slowly and its results accumulate over time. This means that a PR career suits people who are patient and – if they believe in what they are advocating – possess conviction. If you are by nature inclined to want to make a 'big hit' quickly, PR is not the best way to achieve it – as a rule.

Here again, we are trying to point out what is likely to please you, if you are thinking of a career in PR, and what might disappoint you or frustrate you. These are generalisations and there are numerous exceptions. But – in general – PR is known to achieve formidable effects on how people feel and behave, and can change public opinion by 180 degrees – but these effects are rarely spectacular.

As the Lithuanian quantum mechanics expert said, PR secures its most dramatic effects when people can't see that PR is involved at all. Does this kind of 'behind the scenes' work attract you? If so, you could find PR fascinating and rewarding. If not, a different kind of career might be more suited to what you want out of life.

PR work is fast-paced and sometimes frenetic. It's always exciting. It can be quite a rush, in both senses of the word. You have to be able to stay calm. It's occasionally stressful, but most PR people expect this and take it in their stride. On the other hand, it's a collegiate environment to work in – you learn a lot from senior people and colleagues. You really do feel that 'we're all in this together'. The best thing about PR is seeing your ideas working – you can actually see what your work is achieving.

Ben Steele, Communications Officer at Sightsavers

Checklist: Is PR Right for You?

Probably YES

I am curious about current affairs, what's going on and why.

I read a lot – online media, MSM, SocMe, magazines, books.

I like writing. I think I am a good writer. I want to be a better writer.

I am interested in human behaviour – Psychology? History? Sociology?

I like knowing things and sharing what I know with my friends.

I am happy talking but I am also a sponge when other people are talking.

I prefer to spend my spare time doing things with other people.

I know a lot about my favourite subjects.

I do quite well in general knowledge quizzes.

I would describe myself as a sociable person – I have a lot of friends.

I am/was involved in several university clubs or groups.

I want to make my mark in whatever career I choose.

I am a team player and I don't need to be the star of the show.

I am happy to work in the background.

I don't much care if clients take the credit for my ideas and writing.

I am ready to see the effects of my work take effect over time.

I don't mind staying late or coming in early when there's a rush on.

I am usually calm, cool and collected in a panic.

The most important thing to me about work is my colleagues.

Probably NO

I like to work quietly, on my own, without interruptions.

I'm not so keen on socializing with my co-workers.

Rules and clear procedures mean a lot to me.

I don't really like surprises. I want to know what to expect.

I prefer to work set hours with no deviations.

I don't read much. I never saw the point.

> *I can write well enough, but I don't much like adjectives.*
>
> *Social media's OK, of course, but not really for me.*
>
> *I like badminton, but not team games.*
>
> *I don't really think about the salary. It's the pension that matters.*

This may be enough to give you an idea of whether or not you are likely to enjoy PR and be a success in PR. It's pretty clear, from what our experts tell us, that people with curiosity and writing skills are a natural fit for the PR and communications industry. They also tell us that people who prefer an organised, predictable working day might be happier doing something else.

Useful rules of thumb. But please remember, that's all they are – there are lots of exceptions to every rule, and many, many in such a diverse profession as PR.

Why and How I Went into PR

I studied literature at university. I liked reading and writing. When I left I looked for a job involving writing – what I was good at. I worked as a freelance journalist for a while and then I found an opportunity to work as part of a team, which was what I'd always wanted.

Ben Steele, Communications Officer at Sightsavers

I studied political communications at university. I knew what I wanted to do – I grew up in a media family, where I learned a bit about how to write news stories. Then I worked in a four-star hotel, and that taught me a lot about managing client relationships and making sales calls. I think any experience – *any* – can be useful for someone thinking of a PR career.

Stuart McBride is head of PR for a financial trade association

A career in PR suits someone like me with a natural affinity for storytelling, communication and the news. If you like building and nurturing relationships, this career is for you. Success is grounded in the deep and long-term relationships we build with clients, media and the audiences we are targeting.

Virginia Hawkins, PR Consultant at Screaming Frog

I was good at English at school. I decided I wanted a career using the language skills I had and enjoyed. Media? Advertising? PR? I heard a talk about PR from a professor at Bournemouth and made my choice. My colleagues at CCGroup have all kinds of degrees and qualifications. It doesn't really matter – if you feel drawn to PR and have an aptitude, you will probably never look back. I didn't.

Rich Fogg, CEO of CCGroup

If you are at school – don't worry: your future job probably doesn't yet exist! I suggest you keep up with the news and think of your youth as a marketable advantage ... there is a big appetite at agencies and the brands they look after for people who really understand what younger people are thinking, feeling and saying. There is no single path into PR. No real gateways or barriers. I always knew, somehow, that it was the right thing for me. Now I travel all over the world advising companies and brands on their PR. I was right.

Ann-Marie Blake is a well-known PR consultant, advisor and educator

I went into PR from journalism, as many do. The first thing that hit me was how much more time you have in PR to research things properly. Most journalism just skims the surface – it has to – but in PR you can explore further and go into things in much more depth. People sometimes say that PR is superficial, but in my experience it's the exact opposite. There are lots of people like me who have switched from the media to PR and enjoyed the scope they were given to get a real understanding of their clients' industries.

Luke Blair, Director of Communications at an NHS hospital group

I was only good at one thing – writing – so I was hoping for a career in the media. In those days young reporters weren't paid very much. Then this new thing called 'public relations' appeared on my radar. Writing, with a commercial angle. For me, it was the ideal choice. But I have to admit I'm one of those who 'fell into PR' by accident.

Adrian Wheeler, Former CEO of Sterling PR and GCI
Europe

3

THE CORE SKILLS YOU NEED
TO HAVE – OR ACQUIRE

You have read a lot about what makes people suited for a career in public relations and communications, and what makes them happy and successful. Now we'll examine the abilities and aptitudes you need in a bit more depth.

We'll divide these attributes into *interpersonal skills* – how you deal with other people – and *practical skills* – the technical capabilities you need to work in PR and communications.

INTERPERSONAL SKILLS

Do you make a good personal impression on people you meet? *Do you want to?* Let's discuss what this means.

Some of us have the gift of being liked and valued by everyone we encounter. (I am saying 'we' but I don't include myself – I am talking about my friends and colleagues.) What makes these people more memorable and likeable than the rest of us?

It's possible they resemble Jessica Chastain or Matthew Mac-fadyen, but probably not. It's more likely they convince the person they're talking to that they have a deep and genuine interest in that person. We are all more interested in ourselves than anything else, for obvious reasons, so anyone who seems to share that interest will make a strong impression.

Being a Good Listener

A big factor in this is *listening*. 'Being a good listener.' We all listen to other people, all the time, so what's the difference? I think it means focussing *entirely* on what the other person is saying, to the exclusion of everything else. It means taking a real, serious interest in what the other person is trying to say, why they're saying it, what they are really like and what it's like to be them.

This is sometimes called 'empathy'. You either have it or you don't. You can't fake it (unless you're a psychopath, in which case PR is *definitely* not for you). Some people try pretending to be empathetic, but they give themselves away – you spot them looking over your shoulder for someone more important while they're simulating interest in your conversation.

We all know the experience of talking to someone who seems to understand exactly what we're saying and wants to know more about us. This might be a fleeting conversation at a party or a longer interaction in a professional setting. Either way, the conversation makes us feel good. This is what is meant, I suggest, by a 'good listener'.

Is this you? Most of the people I have met in my PR career are 'good listeners' first and foremost. I don't think I have ever met a successful PR person who wasn't. Some of them are very good talkers, too – but when you think about it, what most of us want, most of the time, is to be listened to rather than talked at.

Can you learn it? I'm not sure, but I doubt it. You are either fascinated and intrigued by what makes other people tick, or you're not. If you are – and you might not even be aware that you are – you'll enjoy hearing other people tell you what it's like to be them … their problems, their triumphs, their ambitions and aspirations … maybe even their hopes and dreams, their personal tragedies and disappointments.

If this is you, you not only have an instinctive interest in psychology – the basis for working out how to communicate and connect with other people – but you also have a natural gift for engaging with other human beings, face-to-face, voice-to-voice and screen-to-screen.

Organisational Ability

Other interpersonal skills matter. For instance, you need to be much better organised than most other people. There is so much going on, and it's not usually linear or predictable ... PR people talk about having to 'keep a lot of balls in the air', and PR work can often seem like juggling.

You need to be very patient and accommodating. PR is a *service business*. Your clients and bosses can be infuriating ... your plan is ready, costed and just waiting to go ... *still* the green light or sign-off seems to be delayed ... *why?* The answer is that clients and bosses have other things on their minds. PR is important to them, but it's rarely their Number One priority. (Unless they have a crisis on their hands ... that's different.)

Developing Trust and Confidence

Don't be surprised if your clients or bosses sometimes seem nervous and risk-averse. This can puzzle PR people, but it's normal ... if they never say anything interesting or challenging, nothing bad will happen. They hope. Most senior people are unfamiliar with the ways of the media and can easily feel that the *downside risk* of media coverage outweighs the *upside benefit*. This is a generalisation, like so much in this book. Some clients love media exposure and can't wait to be interviewed; others, especially in corporate and business-to-business PR, can be more circumspect – particularly if they haven't had much experience with the media.

We can understand it. It will be *their* face and name on the screen (not ours) and *their* reputation – and maybe career – which will suffer if something goes wrong.

With clients and bosses like this, we need to gradually win their confidence and persuade them, bit by bit, that stepping off the well-beaten pathway is by far the best way to win positive attention for their company, product or brand. If you are a good listener, you will gain this confidence and trust much more quickly.

What else? Lots, but for now we'll just mention one attribute of successful PR people that could be worth remembering.

Positivity

We never say 'No'.

Instead, we say 'Yes ... and'.

Our client or boss comes up with a so-so idea. We don't want to disappoint them by ruling it out ... but we don't need to. We say: 'Yes ... and ...'.

Then we gradually add to their concept, changing it bit by bit, turning it into something that *we* know will work. If we get this right, everyone's happy. It's just diplomacy.

Sincerity and Truth

You have to be *genuine* if you work in PR. We are sometimes called 'spin-doctors' but this is a travesty favoured by some elements of the media, mainly in political PR. In real life, PR people deal with the truth and only the truth.

They have to, whether they want to or not. The Public Relations and Communications Association Code requires truthfulness, and anyone who chooses to ignore that rule risks being expelled from our professional body (like Bell Pottinger) and will probably (like Bell Pottinger) go out of business shortly afterwards.

However, there are many ways of presenting a client's case, or cause, or product, or claim to fame, in a favourable, positive light – without departing from the truth. It's worth mentioning here that the media never forgive or forget being told a lie, whether by PR people or their clients. If they suspect they have been hood-winked, their relationship with that PR person will never be the same, and is very likely to end there and then.

Handling Disappointment and Frustration

PR people need to be resilient. Nothing is guaranteed ... PR *can* deliver incredible results, with fabulous return on investment (ROI) – or our work *can* fall completely flat. There's a lot of risk involved. A launch we have spent three months preparing can be blotted out by news of a tsunami, a terrorist outrage, a major government statement that no-one was expecting, the arrest of a celebrity, a major launch by our client's biggest competitor ... *anything* can happen, and all our work blows away like confetti.

> You need to be an excellent communicator. Of course! This is a skill you will use every day – both with your clients and your colleagues. Running parallel with this is being an *active listener* with the capability to read the reactions of the room – or your client – and adjust accordingly. This is all about being socially aware and human.
>
> Other skills include crisp copywriting and producing captivating content for various audiences and industries because – trust me – you will work across a lot. You need a can-do attitude. You may work on some of the most exciting consumer brands out there and find your niche in business-to-consumer communications (B2C). Or (if you're like me) you'll be presented with a new client in an industry you don't have much knowledge of but absolutely love working with. A can-do attitude will bring these opportunities your way ... it's crucial to always say 'yes' because you never know where your passion(s) may lie.
>
> The list could go on ... I'll just add that you also need to be approachable and have a keen eye for detail.
>
> *Chloe Baker, Strategy Director at Liquid, an integrated communications consultancy*

Giving Advice and Recommendations

Are you a naturally persuasive person? We mentioned this before – it's a key attribute of people who are good at PR and enjoy it. Do you like giving advice? Do you enjoy knowing about the latest, the best and the newest before your friends, and telling them what to buy, where to go, what to see and who to follow? If not, it's not a problem. But, if so, you could be a PR person by nature. It means you have a natural affinity for the kind of work which PR people do every day of the week.

By the way, *persuasive* does **not** mean argumentative. The opposite. Can you remember the last time someone made you change your mind about something? How did they do it? It's very unlikely that they beat you about the head with arguments until you gave in. It's much more likely that they *listened* to what you said, gently presented an alternative point of view, *listened* to what you said in response, said one or two things about their point of view, *listened* to what you said in reply and then left you to make up your own mind.

What else? You're a good listener, you are fascinated by what makes people the way they are – and they can tell that by talking to you – you're patient but determined ... you may even be lucky enough to have 'charm'.

You Need a Lot of Energy

Energy is important. It's important in most careers, of course, but it's specially valuable in PR, where the hours can be long, the pressure can be high and the challenges can stack up. PR people need to be *determined* and able to draw on reserves of drive, patience and fortitude to carry them through these difficult patches. Even when things are relatively quiet, PR and communications is fast-paced. To be successful, you need a lot of *energy* and, of course, you need to look after your physical and mental well-being.

That's a quick survey of the principal interpersonal skills and personal attributes that most successful PR and communications practitioners seem to possess. Now let's talk briefly about the practical skills and technical abilities that will be useful if you go into PR.

REPUTATION MANAGEMENT

PR is a *professional business service* that delivers specific results to employers or clients. This can broadly be defined as *reputation management*. We are all sensitive to reputation when we decide what to do with our time and money. We don't want to buy products from companies we feel unsure about. We avoid brands owned by companies who, in one way or another, don't measure up to our personal standards. We are either happy, or not very happy, about people in the public eye; whether we support them or don't is mainly a matter of what we know and feel about their reputation.

Reputation is largely controlled by the media and similar third-party sources of information and advice. Presenting our clients and employers to these arbiters of public opinion in a favourable manner forms a large part of what PR and communications professionals are paid to do. How do they do it?

Why Reputation Matters So Much

Reputation is super-important in human affairs, as we all know. It is also massively important in business affairs, and there are figures to prove it.

Thirty years ago most of the value of big companies consisted of things you could touch and count – plant, machinery, buildings, vehicle-fleets, inventory in warehouses ... and so on.

Today, most of the value of big companies – about 80 per cent – is attributable to things you cannot see or touch – popular brands, a well-liked chief executive officer (CEO), a 'good image', a solid 'licence to operate', goodwill, strong relationships with distributors and suppliers, consumer and stakeholder approval ... in other words 'a good reputation'.

Most CEOs consider protecting and enhancing corporate reputation as a top priority. It's what keeps them awake at night. It's their personal responsibility: they receive credit when the company distinguishes itself and take the blame when things go badly wrong. At the same time, they know they can't see and control everything 24×7×52.

'Protecting and enhancing reputation' is what PR and communications professionals focus on day in and day out.

What does 'reputation' mean? We all know, in a general way ... acceptable, admired, 'in good standing', popular, well-liked, reliable, trustworthy, in line with commonly accepted tenets and values ... for investors it means something more: 'a company I feel confident supporting with my and my client's money' ... for consumers it can mean something a bit different: 'a company or brand that I will feel pleased and even proud to own' ... for business partners it means other things, for banks other things again ... 'reputation' has slightly different implications for every stakeholder group you can think of. But in the end, it's the same thing.

We can measure reputational assets as they increase (or decline) over time. There is a direct mathematical correlation between reputational assets and commercial success.

Reputation is super-important and it's also fragile. It all depends on what people feel and think. That's one reason why reputation management – the work of PR and communications professionals – is so fascinating and rewarding ... it's difficult.

A reputation takes years to build and can be lost overnight.

Thirty years ago, big companies didn't have to pay very much attention to what ordinary people thought or felt. Since 2000, when internet access began to be universal, all that changed. Reputation today depends on interaction ... 'the conversation'. That's where professional PR and communications people have so much of value to contribute.

PRACTICAL SKILLS

You know what comes first. *Writing!*

Human communication is much more about feelings and emotions than facts. Successful *persuasive communication* is a skilful blend of both.

Good journalism *feeds the mind and touches the heart*. Even if your topic is factual and serious, you won't get anyone to take it in and remember it unless you *also* arouse some kind of emotional response. This is the basis of curiosity.

Feelings matter much more than *facts* when we are trying to be persuasive. Emotions count for much more than intellectual ability or intelligence.

We know this from research in Behavioural Economics, which is well on the way to turning PR and communications from a *slightly mysterious art* into a fact-based combination of *scientific knowledge and creative talent.*

Many of the attributes I see in PR professionals are similar to those of our journalist colleagues – you need that innate curiosity and drive to deliver on your story. The added factor – or complication – is the client. To effectively balance the wishes of your client and the requirements of a journalist, PR professionals need a level of flexibility and diplomacy ... it can be a difficult line to walk.

Oli Higgs, Senior PR Consultant with
Speed Communications

Adaptability, creativity and continuous improvement ... mastering these will lead to a long and successful career.

Virginia Hawkins, PR Consultant at Screaming Frog

WHY ARE WRITING SKILLS SO IMPORTANT IN PR AND COMMUNICATIONS?

It's very hard to write in a way that makes readers want to continue 'hearing' what you have to say. *You could tell me that this book demonstrates that fact, but I hope not.* Catching and holding a reader's attention (or a listener's, or a viewer's, or a browser's) for long enough to get a message across is challenging. Remember: 4,000 other messages every day.

It's all about conveying the key facts *briefly and concisely* with enough emotional 'hooks' to keep people reading. Sounds simple ... but isn't.

The master of short, sharp, unadorned, terse, vivid prose was Ernest Hemingway. He took hours and sometimes days to compose a single paragraph. We can't do that! Nor can journalists.

We somehow have to compress all that needs to be said into a very few words, so that – with any luck – our audience will carry on reading and take what we're saying on board. Most people are impatient when they're reading the media, and move on to the next story quickly – unless our writing has drawn them in. This is where writing talent is at a premium.

Some people are born with it. Their names are famous and we buy their books. Most of us have this ability to some extent. All of us can improve with training and practice.

Several famous authors are supposed to have started a letter by saying: 'Dear Friend … I am sorry this letter is so long. I did not have time to make it shorter'.

Writing short, concise prose is – by common consent – the single most valuable technical skill for a successful PR and communications person.

THINKING IN PICTURES

Visualization. We live in a world where images are more and more important. Illustrations, photography, infographics, footage, clips … in a PR career you will have specialists to help you with imagery, of course … but do you normally think in visual terms, or are you more likely to think in words?

Can you combine the two?

Some of the most eminent innovators in science and the arts are said to think in images rather than words. Can we train ourselves to think in pictures and concepts – rather than words alone?

When we're writing for publication we also need to be able to visualise how the item will look on the screen, or on the page. Or how it will end up sounding on radio or in a podcast. Ernest Hemingway never had to bother about this. But *persuasive communicators* need to pay attention not only to the words but also to how they will appear when published.

Can we be Ridley Scott rather than Jane Austen? Or both at the same time?

WE NEED TO BE GOOD ANALYSTS

Our main purpose in PR and communications is to take information from a variety of sources and turn it into something new and interesting that our media customers want to publish and our audiences want to talk about to each other. This is called 'talkability'. Imagine the famous 'water-cooler conversation'. Are they talking about our client?

The world is awash with information. Most of it is designed to look interesting but fails to come up to our expectations when we read on (or continue listening, watching and browsing). This is one reason why people rarely finish consuming media items – they typically click away or scroll down part-way through, switching off either literally or figuratively.

Good writers (or composers of content) know how to pick out the key components from their sources and assemble them into short, cogent, impactful pieces of copy. This isn't easy and it takes time. Successful PR people usually have a 'news instinct' – just like journalists. They get better and better at it as their careers progress.

IT HELPS TO BE GOOD AT MATHS

People who are *very* good at maths usually go into engineering, architecture, economics or one of the sciences. There aren't many PR people with degrees in quantum mechanics.

But, even if maths isn't your favourite subject, it's extremely useful in a PR career. This is because nearly all clients and employers are organisations, and organisations are usually financial entities. Numbers really matter, so if you want to talk the same language as your clients and employers it's a good idea to be numerate.

At a more basic level, every project or programme you're involved in will have a budget. One of your managers or directors will have worked out, in great detail, how the budget will be allocated over the lifetime of the campaign. Actual expenditure has to be monitored as the programme rolls out. Once you're a manager yourself, this will be your responsibility.

There are lots of metrics enabling PR people and their clients to measure ROI. These are all mathematical and are displayed as spreadsheets, graphs and charts. You will need to be familiar with these systems and how to operate them.

MAKING JUDGEMENTS QUICKLY

We are part of the media world in PR and communications, and the media world moves fast. If you've visited a newsroom you were probably struck by the speed and noise when deadlines were approaching. It's similar in a PR agency or department, though luckily for us the pace and pressure are not so relentless.

What this means is that we often need to make snap judgements. Sometimes we have plenty of time to research, think and discuss, but sometimes we have to make decisions on the spur of the moment – or risk getting left behind.

It also means that sometimes we'll be wrong. For PR people, that's just an opportunity to learn something new and move on.

MINI-PRACTICAL

Here's a fictional scenario. Like a lot of small companies, the client relies on PR rather than advertising to communicate with its target audiences.

We work for a small printer company – a challenger brand. They get very little media attention because they are competing with famous manufacturers like Epson, HP and Brother. It's an uphill struggle.

They've just told us that they are launching a new printer in three months. This one has a compelling USP (Unique Selling Proposition): its ink cartridges cost the same as everyone else's but last twice as long.

There's a slight catch: the printer itself costs 50 per cent more.

Our client has a value-for-money argument and a story about innovation. We can see a theme about long duration and another about convenience at work. (Say goodbye to frequent ink cartridge replacement misery!) We are tempted to compare our client to Dyson (more expensive but much better).

How would you visualise the story-platform that will introduce this new printer to the world?

Creativity in Action

Our agency's client was opening a new logistics park (ware-houses) near Swindon. They were very proud of their green credentials and were hoping for major coverage ... but it was a logistics park like a hundred others. Nothing special, no obvious story.

Then one of us had a brilliant idea. She arranged for a grassy area to be laid down in the middle of the warehouses. In the middle of the grassy area, she had a small pond dug, with a few reeds and bullrushes.

On the day of the official opening, the Mayor turned up expecting to cut a ribbon as usual. But instead he pulled a lever which opened the door of a cage. Two ducks waddled out, across the grass and into the pond.

This simple idea had 'charm' which made the media love it. Our client got wall-to-wall coverage in the locals, trades and regional TV. The ducks were liked and shared thousands of times.

Successful PR sometimes means producing a new idea out of thin air.

Is PR Like Journalism?

PR and the media are like brothers and sisters – they share a lot in common but the relationship can vary from 'very close' to 'daggers drawn'.

We all do much the same thing: produce content which is meant to inform, enlighten and entertain specific groups within the general public – sometimes everyone.

Journalists are not well-paid, unless they are one of the few who become big names. PR people are paid more. Journalists think of themselves as true professionals, whereas they think of PR people as the hired servants of capitalism, politics or interest-groups.

Journalists consider themselves to be guardians of the public interest. They are drawn to campaigns, crusades and movements which set out to expose wrongdoing. They are encouraged to challenge the establishment, to 'speak truth to power'.

Journalists sometimes joke that bad news is good news and good news isn't news at all. It's not really a joke. They can sometimes be heard to say: 'Why let the facts get in the way of a good story?' but they don't mean it.

I have known hundreds of journalists and most of them would sooner die than report a falsehood. But there are rare exceptions.

What happened to the 20,000 journalists who left the media industry since 2000? Some of them went into PR. A few did very well. Many didn't. If you're a journalist you have power (though they very rarely mention it). In PR we can have influence, but not power. For some journalists 'crossing to the dark side' was no fun at all.

Most of what appears in today's media originates in PR departments and PR agencies. Very few journalists like this state of affairs, but they are stuck with it.

Some *really* don't like it. They can often treat PR people harshly, and even aggressively, for no apparent reason.

Most people working in PR admire journalism, respect journalists in general (some more than others) and have good working relationships with as many as possible. We want them to see us as fellow-professionals, sometimes on opposite sides of a case – like lawyers – but ready to have a friendly drink in the pub afterwards. They can see us as well-paid barriers to the truth, or as useful allies in the performance of their work.

Journalists, reporters, editors and correspondents matter to people in PR. They are genuine third-party sources of information and opinion. You can fire up a bot to swamp social media with 'news' and you can pay an influencer thousands to say nice things about your client's fashion brand, cake-mix, lipstick or car. We all know it's advertising. But when a journalist says something ... we take it as the unalloyed truth.

We all do. Are we right? here's what Humbert Wolfe wrote in 1930:

> You cannot hope to bribe or twist.
>
> Thank God, the British journalist.
>
> But seeing what the man will do
>
> Unbribed, there's no occasion to.

It *can* be a tense and confrontational relationship, but not usually. We need them and they need us. Successful PR people develop a good working relationship with the media. They can even become lifelong friends. In any case, it is an asset in PR to understand the media, like journalists and enjoy their company.

Getting Your Media Writing Published Is Difficult

Editors divide media material into 'hard news' (we have to publish this) and 'soft news' (we'll use it if we have the space or time). If we are handling a really big story for our client (hard news) it will be easy enough to attract the media's attention. But most of the time we're not. Most of the time we're trying to interest the media in stories where they have a choice – it won't matter to them if our story gets spiked.

Professor Trevor Morris (Westminster and Richmond Universities) taught his PR and communications students the 'Iron Law'. It's usually possible to get a story published somewhere. But that's not what employers and clients want. They want their story to appear in the most important and influential outlets (and so do we). The Iron Law says that the harder it is to get a story accepted, the more useful it will be to the client, and vice versa.

A very early pioneer of UK PR, back in the 1920s, said that a typical article submitted to the newspapers only had a one in a hundred chance of being published. Nothing's changed: we still have only a one per cent chance, on average, of getting our story published in an outlet where we, and our client, want to see it.

PR is very competitive. To succeed we need persistence and that 'can-do' attitude Chloe Baker recommended. We also need good 'news sense' and the ability to present stories to our media customers in a manner that attracts their interest and that they see as helpful in the performance of their work.

Some journalists build their whole careers on connections with PR people. It's symbiotic: getting exclusive information via a PR person saves time and effort. Explaining why a story matters and where the information comes from is sometimes easier for a journalist when it's backed by a well-regarded PR person. I should also mention that a close connection to a PR person can open an exit path for journalists who want to change sides' and start over in PR.

Dr Carsten Priebe is an award-winning financial journalist, analyst and author

4

THE PR AND COMMUNICATIONS LANDSCAPE

As you know, public relations (PR) and communications is now a major professional business services industry. According to the Public Relations and Communications Association (PRCA), there are nearly 100,000 people working in PR and communications and close to £15 billion is invested in PR annually in the United Kingdom alone.

If you are thinking about (or wondering about) a career in PR and communications, it may be helpful to have an idea of the 'landscape' – the shape of the industry – and something about the various fauna that inhabit it.

Some people say that PR goes back to the dawn of history. They might be joking, but it's clear that kings and emperors have always tried hard to leave their own version of events for later generations to read and remember.

There are temples all over Egypt recording the triumphs of pharaohs thousands of years ago. They are still visible today, so they have achieved longevity. But are they true historical accounts? Most archaeologists raise an eyebrow – these carvings fail the credibility test.

There are tens of thousands of books written by political and military leaders over the centuries, all telling their story from their own point of view, showing themselves in the best possible light. This is certainly a variety of *persuasive communication*.

But it isn't PR as we know it today.

LIKE ADVERTISING, PR FIRST DEVELOPED
IN THE UNITED STATES

We saw earlier that modern PR emerged in the United States in the early years of the 20th century. Big companies and brands were quick to see that attractive ideas, disseminated through the media, could do wonders for their reputations and sales. In those days 'the media' meant local newspapers, with a bit of local radio. PR as an industry – like advertising – really only took off once *national* media – radio and TV – made it possible for companies (and governments) to talk to everyone at once.

Here in the United Kingdom, there were a few fledgling PR pioneers like Basil Clarke in the 1920s, but PR as a recognised commercial discipline only got going after the Second World War, and even then remained a small and specialist business sector until the 1970s. The UK industry has grown steadily ever since, with a strong boost around 2000, when digital communication became available and affordable to millions.

Britain has proved to be fertile ground for the PR and communications industry. We have very large numbers of national media in this country – to say nothing of thousands of trade, technical and professional (TTP) outlets and a great variety of local and general interest titles ... by some measures the United Kingdom is the most media-saturated country in the world.

This thriving media market enabled a vigorous (and competitive) PR industry to develop to the point where many international PR experts began to consider the United Kingdom as offering the most sophisticated and creative PR services in the world. Naturally, other countries have not been slow to challenge this position.

One of the wonderful aspects of PR, when you work in the industry, is how quickly new ways of thinking travel around the global PR community. PR people compete like cats-and-dogs, but they also spend a lot of time meeting each other, swapping ideas and sharing thoughts on best practice. There are several international bodies devoted to staging events where PR and communications people can meet, confer and debate – for instance, the International Communications Consultancy Organisation (ICCO), which is managed by our own PRCA.

All that said – the United Kingdom is a great place, and probably the best, to embark on a career in PR.

IS PR ALL ABOUT LONDON?

No. In the early days, most (though not all) national and international agencies were based in London – partly because, in those days, that's where all the media were. Things have changed; I would estimate that half the United Kingdom's PR agencies today have their offices in other large UK cities, and in many cases in smaller towns.

London is still the only place to be if you work in financial communications or government relations. But for corporate, business-to-business (B2B) and brand communications you can work anywhere. London retains its allure for PR people as for many other professions, so if you can afford to live there, or travel there (assuming your employer wants you in the office), it's definitely worth thinking about when you take your first steps in PR and communications. But, if you prefer not to, there are equally good opportunities much nearer to where you live.

CONSULTANCY AND IN-HOUSE

As a very rough estimate, half the PR people in the United Kingdom work in agencies (or consultancies – same thing) and half work 'in-house' – in PR and communications departments within companies, government departments, local authorities, charities, public services and so on. What should you choose? My personal view is that it doesn't matter. You learn PR by doing PR and watching other people do PR, and there isn't much difference between a (good) agency and a (good) in-house department.

Both the 'agency world' and the 'in-house world' invest in training their people. Your pay and benefits won't be very different, because both agencies and in-house departments are competing for the best new recruits. There can be a difference in the workload and pressure – as a rule of thumb, agency life is busier, higher-pressure and often more stressful than life in an in-house department – but there are many exceptions to disprove this rule.

My advice is to think about *what they do*, rather than what the working environment is like. If, for instance, you are mad about airlines, it would make sense to see if you can begin your PR career in an airline's PR department. But if you are mad about politics, you'd probably get a better entrée into political communications in a public affairs consultancy. If you are fascinated by brands and brand communications, you'd learn a lot, quickly, working at a company like Mars. If you're not yet sure which industry would be 'your thing', working in an agency, with exposure to a variety of different clients, could be a useful way to decide on your favoured route.

As I said earlier, it doesn't really make much difference. People switch from agency to in-house, and from in-house to agency, all the time. Some people start their careers in agencies and never want to work anywhere else (though they may well move from one agency to another until they find the one that suits them best). Others have a clear preference for working in-house from the word go ... and then decide to switch after three, five or ten years. Anyone can change their mind at any time in PR and communications. It's a 'war for talent'!

Is it best to start with an agency or in-house? It really doesn't matter. I've debated with my colleagues for years whether the *real* professional communicators are in agencies, where they think about nothing but communications all day long, or in-house, where people tend to see the wider picture.

In some ways the in-house environment can be slightly less competitive, and it's usually much less commercially-focussed. But I've also worked in in-house roles where politics gets in the way, which is much more unusual in the agency world.

Understanding how agencies work can be an advantage if you move in-house later in your career. People who've always worked in-house can make assumptions about PR and communications agencies which are far from the truth. On the other hand, starting in-house will teach you about how organisations *really* work – something I never fully comprehended as a journalist, and which became very useful when I went on to work in consultancies. You are better-placed to understand what makes your clients tick.

One of the many good things about a career in PR is that you will always have this choice – to work in-house, or in an agency, and to switch back and forth between the two. You may also get the chance to be 'seconded' from your agency into a full-time, but temporary, role within a client. This can mean the best of both worlds!

Luke Blair, Director of Communications at an NHS hospital group

ARE LARGE OR SMALL AGENCIES BETTER?

Another rule of thumb: it's not the *agency* that matters most – it's the team you work in, and how good your boss is.

Clients know this: when they're choosing agencies (consultancies) they pay more attention to the *people they are meeting* than to the size and credentials of the agency they work for. Clients usually see agencies as a 'portal' they go through, hoping to meet a small team of people who will (they hope) make all the difference to the profile of their brand or company.

If I can offer any advice here, it would be to avoid preconceptions. PR is still a fairly new profession, evolving year by year ... not much is fixed ... a firm that was the 'hot' place to work last year can be (for example) taken over this year and turn into a media mill ... a firm that had a reputation as a sweat-shop can hire a new chief executive officer (CEO) this year who transforms it into the Best Place To Work. The PR industry is not like accountancy ... it changes while you're looking the other way. Some people find this annoying. I don't. You?

GENERAL PRACTICE AND SPECIALISED AGENCIES

Here are some more signposts to help you if you are considering a career in PR.

If you feel that life in a *PR agency* would be more to your liking – at least to start with – you need to decide which kind of agency to aim for. As well as being small, medium and large, and as well as being London-based or somewhere else, agencies (also known as consultancies) can be divided into *general practice* firms and *specialists*.

General practice firms – which includes most of the medium-sized and large companies – contain specialist teams (for example, consumer, B2B, tech, healthcare and financial services) whereas in a specialist firm everyone is an expert in one specific industry sector. City agencies offering investor relations support, for instance, *usually* do nothing else. Healthcare agencies may specialise in Rx (prescription medicines) or OTC (branded pharmaceuticals sold 'over the counter') but they don't normally offer communications services to clients outside the specialist realm of healthcare.

Do you have a strong personal interest in a particular industry already? If so, a good plan would be to identify large agencies which have a specialist team concentrating on that industry, plus smaller agencies which focus entirely on it.

If you don't yet know which industry (or industries) you find the most fascinating, it is almost irrelevant which kind of agency (or in-house department) you join. You will soon develop preferences and gradually become a specialist – though your chosen field might be fairly broad (for example, brands and B2C communications) or it could be comparatively narrow (for example, property development, the aeronautical industry, logistics or financial services).

What I love most about my career is the strategic thinking involved. It's not just about writing press releases and pitching stories, but understanding the bigger picture, anticipating audience reactions, and shaping the narrative.

Alexandra Bingham, Senior Media and Communications Officer at Mercy Corps

If you'd like to work in **PR**, start by thinking about what you'd like to do and who you'd like to do it for. Go online and explore the different parts of the industry. Which appeals to you most? Internal communications? Public affairs? Media relations? Digital? Next, think about which sector you'd like to work in. Head back online and start looking at different industries and how they communicate with their key audiences. Does anyone stand out?

Stuart McBride is head of PR for a financial trade association

PR AND COMMUNICATIONS SPECIALISATIONS

There are 500 PR and communications companies in the PRCA, from the very large to the fairly small, covering the whole spectrum from multi-disciplinary to highly specialised. Here is a quick description of the principal 'categories' of PR you are likely to meet.

Corporate Communications and Reputation Management

From the point of view of a newcomer to PR and communications, this 'category' is the least obvious to the naked eye. It means taking responsibility for the totality of an organisation's 'reputational assets' – its good name, credibility, 'positive image', good standing, credibility … compliance with generally accepted standards of behaviour and governance … engagement with decision-makers, opinion-formers, stakeholders and members of the public at large … across the map.

This is regarded as 'heavyweight' PR work and it's very rewarding. It's the area of PR where we are most likely to find ourselves working directly for, or alongside, senior business people, grappling with some of the most complex challenges and issues in corporate life. It calls for analytical skills, wide knowledge and substantial experience.

Financial Communications, Investor Relations and City PR

This is a relatively small 'category' whose practitioners help companies (usually large, usually quoted) present the best narrative of their performance, prospects and leadership to the financial community, and in particular to the managers of investment funds. The role of these experts is always crucial but becomes even more critical in the case of a company's launch (IPO - Initial Public Offering) and in the case of an acquisition, takeover or merger.

City PR appeals to people who are drawn to the world of finance, bids and deals, stocks and shares – the kind of people who read the *Financial Times* or the *Wall Street Journal*. Here, too, these communications experts operate at board level. If you have a good head for numbers and you enjoyed 'The Big Short', this could be the perfect area of PR for you.

Public Affairs, Political Communications and Lobbying

This is the third area of PR and communications that normally involves our clients' chairs and CEOs on a direct, daily basis. It can be summed up as making sure that legislators and regulators have a true and positive picture of our clients' (or employers') positions on any area of legislation or regulation that affects their (usually commercial) activities. This means knowing how to engage with and affect the many advisors and sources of information which senior political figures depend on.

Public affairs has less to do with the media than other forms of PR, and much more to do with personal, face-to-face contact. We will get advice from Lionel Zetter, the public affairs guru, later in this book; for now, it's enough to say that Public Affairs isn't *really* a variety of PR and communications, and is likely to attract you if you have an intense interest in politics.

Internal Communications

This is a highly important speciality whose audiences are the people working for and with our client's organisation. All-round

PR practitioners can, and often do, provide internal communications services – though it's increasingly recognised as a
specialised area, partly PR but more closely allied with human
resources (HR).

The CEO of one of our favourite clients at GCI once said
to us:

> *The main difference between us and our competitors is the*
> *quality of the people we recruit, how happy we can make*
> *them while they're working with us, and how long they*
> *stay at our company. Can you help us with that?*

Community Engagement and Good Corporate Citizenship

This area of PR consultancy can sound nebulous but is actually
highly important and becoming more so with every year that
passes. We all want to buy things from, and work with, companies
and brands that we approve of and feel in some way happy with.
We take active steps to avoid contact with companies and brands
which, we feel, fall short on things like integrity, fair dealing, equi-
table employment policies and playing a responsible role in the
community at large.

All PR consultancies and departments – I think without
exception – are called on to advise their clients and employers on
how to present themselves in this acceptable, and ideally favourable, light. It's an important source of *competitive advantage*. To
cite one high-profile example … fashion brands are often accused
of employing underpaid and even under-age labour to make their
products in countries where jobs of any kind are scarce. These
brands need policies which their customers know about, understand and believe in.

This area of PR and communications work is sometimes
referred to as *corporate social responsibility* (CSR) or *corporate
social investment* (CSI). It has close links with with environmental,
social, governance (ESG) and equity, diversity, inclusion (EDI) and
often entails *corporate philanthropy, corporate and brand outreach*
and *cause-related marketing*.

When the Toy Industry Had No Friends or Supporters

Our firm was hired by the trade association of the British toy industry because they faced the imposition of a watershed on TV advertising. We began by researching the decision-makers and opinion-formers in the legislative and regulatory groups that made the rules.

We found that no-one liked the toy industry. They were seen as 'cowboys' who caused death and injury to children in the pursuit of profit. This was strange, because British toy industry standards of safety and quality were the highest in the world, and had been copied by many other countries.

The problem was that no-one – parents, childcare experts, MPs, academics, journalists – could tell the difference between toys made by our clients' members and counterfeits sold on market-stalls.

The solution began with a safety-symbol – The Lion Mark. Our clients were gradually able to introduce themselves to all the people whose opinions mattered, and present the industry as what is really was – a model of good corporate citizenship.

Within two years the toy industry had won friends and advocates at all levels. It became a business sector of which UK PLC could be justifiably proud.

B2C, Consumer and Brand Communications

This is what most people think of when they think of PR. Favourable reviews, celebrity endorsements, influencers, high-profile media 'stunts', the battle for prominence in retail outlets and online, brand ambassadors, sponsorship, product placement in movies and TV series ... most people would think of business-to-consumer (B2C) as the most exciting and enjoyable area of PR. Think of working for Red Bull or Virgin ... Primark, Rolex, Croatia, etc.

The creativity is what catches our eye, but it's only the tip of the iceberg. Managing brands is a highly evolved science – fascinating to learn, and you'll need to know something about it when you talk to your clients' marketing directors and brand managers. This area of PR is also where you're most likely to find yourself working alongside experts in advertising, direct marketing, sponsorship, 'presence marketing' and ambient media.

There is a dividing line between B2C and B2B PR, but it's very porous. Many PR people and agencies cover both, and a typical PR career will see you working in B2C, then B2B, then back again in B2C, before – perhaps – concentrating on one or the other.

B2B – PR and Communications

This sector is where our clients or employers are providing products and services to customers and clients working in a professional capacity. For instance, if we make airliners our customers are highly qualified individuals employed by airlines, or perhaps by leasing companies. Our clients or employers could be making products that consumers have never heard of and don't care about – for example, the insulation that makes cars quieter and more comfortable for passengers.

I've sometimes heard people say that B2B is dull by comparison with B2C, but this is wrong. It's just as competitive – in some ways even more so – and effective PR relies just as much on attractive, creative ideas – even though the facts and figures are usually more salient than in B2C marketing communications.

To succeed in B2B PR you need to know your client's products or services inside out – you must be nearly as knowledgeable as the B2B journalists you are talking to. Some people find acquiring this in-depth knowledge very satisfying, and if this sounds like you, it's likely that you would enjoy a career in B2B PR and communications.

Specialist Industry Sectors

Whether corporate, B2C or B2B, there are some industries where PR people need real, specialist knowledge if they are going to be able to understand what their clients are saying, let alone represent those clients with expert media and other stakeholders.

Healthcare is an obvious example. There are some PR people who found their way into healthcare communications, but many more who were educated and trained in some area of healthcare (for example, biochemistry, pharmacy and microbiology) and then found their way into PR.

Tech is another. Clients and employers in information technology expect their PR advisors to possess deep technical knowledge. This can be acquired 'on the job', and often is, but a science degree can be a big advantage. Mark Adams, who co-founded the biggest tech PR consultancy in the world, studied physics at Reading and then went straight into PR. It's not essential to follow his example, but it helps.

The same applies, to varying degrees, in other fields whose stock-in-trade is knowledge. Banking and financial services need PR people who understand the intricacies of the financial markets. If your client is in logistics, you need to know at least the basics of freight-forwarding, shipping, air cargo, rail and road transport and storage. A client developing offices, residential estates, retail malls or industrial wants their PR advisors to know exactly how the planning system works, and how 'placemaking' is at the heart of successful marketing to potential buyers or tenants.

The list goes on ... as a general rule, PR and communications people working for clients in highly specialised sectors need highly specialised knowledge. There are many exceptions, because you *can* learn what you need to know while working, but – as a general rule – it's very useful to start with some kind of qualification or experience in your client's sector.

International PR and Communications

Are you attracted by the idea of working in other countries? If so, PR and communications is one of the professional areas where you would find this easy to achieve, specially if you have mastered a foreign language.

The large agencies are all international and have offices everywhere. They very often move people about, partly because this is a good way to give rising stars valuable experience. But international opportunities are not restricted to the big firms; medium-sized and even small firms may belong to a voluntary group (a kind of international association or partnership of independent agencies), and these can give you the chance to work abroad on a temporary or even permanent basis.

If you find yourself in charge of a multi-country PR programme at a later stage in your career, experience of working in other countries is, obviously, very valuable. You don't need us to tell you that people think, work and behave very differently from one country to the next – but you'd be surprised how often a 'one-size-fits-all' marketing plan ignores this fact. If you have international experience behind you, you'll be well-placed to make sure your clients or employers tailor their marketing very precisely to the characteristics of each country, region or locality where they are hoping to sell something.

How to Tell Which Agencies Are Large, Medium-sized and Small?

If you decide you want to begin your PR career working at an agency, you'll need to know which ones are specialists, which are generalists, which are international, which are small, where they are located ... you need a list.

PR Week *publishes an annual league table of the top 150 agencies in the United Kingdom. If you can get hold of a copy, this is a useful way to start.*

Look at the PRCA's website. The Membership Directory gives the names of agencies (and in-house departments) with links to their websites.

Most websites not only tell you all you need to know about the agency but also have dedicated careers sections for potential recruits.

You're probably already familiar with Glassdoor. Worth checking out.

MINI-PRACTICAL

Here's a fictional scenario.

You work for a medium-sized PR consultancy with a broad mix of clients across corporate, B2C and B2B. You joined two years ago and are doing well. The firm is based in Manchester but its clients are all over the United Kingdom, with a small number in the United States and Scandinavia.

The firm is growing and wants to recruit more bright, new staff (people like you) from UK universities. The CEO comes over for a chat; she wants you to head up the recruitment campaign. She tells you that she thinks people with arts or humanities degrees would be best-suited to PR, but she doesn't have a fixed opinion.

Her goal is three new graduates within the next six months.

What will you do? Will you brief the leading recruitment consultancies and wait to see what happens? Or will you think up a PR programme for your PR firm, targeting the kind of media that people like you (as an undergraduate) consumed? Will your campaign be local, regional or national? Think back – how did you find out about the agency you now work for? How did you find them, or they find you?

You can use conventional methods … but what about something totally original?

A career in PR suits people with a natural affinity for storytelling, communication and the news. If you also have an ability to build and nurture relationships, this career is for you. The industry is dynamic and always changing, so being self-critical and having the confidence to be disruptive can also help you succeed.

Virginia Hawkins, PR Consultant at Screaming Frog

5

WORKING IN PR AND COMMUNICATIONS – WHAT IT'S LIKE

Every public relations agency and PR team is different – more so than most other professional business services. There *are* common factors – the importance of the media, the need for creativity, opportunities and problems which arrive without warning, a collegiate approach to doing most things – but every agency or team has its own 'style' and atmosphere, and they can be as different as whiteboard-markers and Wensleydale.

That said, let's try to give a portrait of a typical working day in the life of a typical junior executive in a typical agency somewhere west of London. Ella has been with the firm for just over a year. Her agency is a tech specialist and she's part of the teams looking after two international clients – a digital security company based in Munich and an online fashion retailer based in Toulouse. Ella is a good writer, so she's often asked to help out when other client teams need copy for a news-feature, a speech or a script.

Ella's agency has a 3:2 working from home (WFH) policy, which means Ella can choose to work from home two days a week if her client obligations allow it. Some of her colleagues – specially those with young families – find this WFH policy really useful, but Ella doesn't. She prefers to be in the office alongside more experienced members of the agency, watching and learning, asking questions and getting feedback on her work.

Today Ella gets up early and scans the news while she has her breakfast. Is there anything about online security or fashion retail? Any announcements by her clients' competitors, any economic forecasts, any government policy statements which could affect their business? If so, Ella will alert her account manager – should we let the client know and suggest a course of action? Ella's agency makes a point of knowing what's in the news before their clients do, and coming up with proactive ideas to solve a problem or exploit an opportunity.

CLIENT REVIEW MEETING

Today starts with a meeting of the team working on the digital security account. The account director, the account manager and Ella are all in the office, while the account executive joins the meeting online from home. The point of the meeting is to agree on the highlights of this month's monthly report and discuss the programme for the month ahead. As it happens, the coming month is going to be very busy because the client is attending an important trade show and two people from the agency will need to be there to manage media interaction, but everyone also puts a date in their schedule for a team meeting later in the month to come up with some new ideas and initiatives for the next quarter.

Ella loves these idea meetings. Even though she's the youngest person in the team, her suggestions are taken seriously and often get adopted as part of the proposal. Her account director says she has a good perspective, because of her age, on how young entrepreneurs think about digital security.

After the meeting, Ella goes back to her desk to work on a press release for another client entirely – an online car auction site. They want to capture pole position in the UK market for used electric vehicles. This means an hour or so researching what other second-hand car dealers and auctioneers are saying. Ella knows that the client needs a point of difference that will stand up to media scrutiny. This is another aspect of her work that Ella enjoys: finding out what's being said and what's being reported, then coming up with an opportunity for the client.

It's not really a 'desk'. Ella's agency has been open-plan since day one, but they've experimented with various layouts and designs. When Ella joined, everyone worked in cubicles divided by shoulder-high partitions. Everybody hated them, so now the whole firm sits at long tables with no screens or panels. If anyone needs peace and quiet to concentrate on something, there are glass boxes all along one wall. There are also two large and two small meeting rooms, and 'The Library'.

A CLIENT BRIEFING

At 11 a.m., the account team assembles in 'The Library' for a Zoom meeting with their online fashion retail client, who is launching a new seasonal range next month and expects it to take the world by storm. Ella was surprised, when she first joined the agency, how fast things moved and changed in the world of tech PR. But online fashion leaves tech standing. It's a challenge to keep up – everything can change overnight – but it's exciting.

Lunchtime: Ella could go out, but the owner of the agency provides lunch every day, at the agency's expense, for everyone who wants to eat in. There's a kitchen with tables and chairs. For Ella, this is a great opportunity to chat with her senior colleagues. She's determined to learn as much as she can, as quickly as she can.

A TRAINING WEBINAR

After lunch, Ella logs on for a one-hour training webinar about pitching stories to the media. It's given by the Public Relations and Communications Association (PRCA). Ella has signed up for the PRCA's Foundation Certificate, which means 'attending' a series of online courses and then writing a set of essays for assessment. Ella's agency is a firm believer in formal training in conjunction with 'learning by doing' and is supporting her. Ella enjoys these training sessions, and she's already decided that *crisis communications* is an area where she wants, in due course, to become something of a specialist.

RECORDING A PODCAST

The founder of the agency's digital security client has been invited onto a cybersecurity podcast. Ella has written key messages and talking points for him. Her team leader has briefed the podcast host, who's in Boston. The client has come to the agency's studio to 'perform'. Ella and her team leader are there to give moral support and advice.

As it turns out, he doesn't need it. He's fluent, concise and to-the-point. He covers off all the key messages. He even makes a few jokes. The host is obviously very pleased. When the client leaves, Ella's team-leader says:

> *Can you believe that was the first podcast he's ever done?*
> *If only all our clients were such naturals in front of a mic.*
> *Let's see what he's like on camera. Ella, could you fix up a*
> *TV media training session for him?*

A TRIP TO MUNICH

The digital security client has an important upgrade to announce. The account director feels that the story needs in-depth explanation, so she recommends that the client should host a small group of UK IT security media experts in Munich. She thinks a whole afternoon and evening will give the client's top people a chance to establish good relationships with the journalists.

Ella will be part of the agency team, mainly because the account director thinks it will give her good experience of handling a 'press trip' and also because it will give her useful exposure to the client. The team has discussed who to invite – there will be six in the party – and how to invite them; they agree that Ella will start by phoning the 'A-List', who all know the agency and have covered the client's stories, to see who's interested and available. She starts by briefing herself on the travel arrangements, the hotel and the restaurant where the client will host their guests from the United Kingdom.

AFTER WORK

By now, it's 5.30 p.m. and people are starting to pack up for the day. It's Tom's third anniversary of joining the firm, so the founder is taking everyone to celebrate at the agency's favourite bar. But Ella and her friend Naomi have an hour in the gym three evenings a week, and this is one of them. 'We'll catch up with you later!'

They did, and had a great time. Six of them went on to a local bistro.

There was always something going on. The next evening, an artificial intelligence expert was coming in at 6 p.m. to give a talk on how large language models (LLMs) were set to change the creative industries. Invitations had gone out to clients, media contacts, friends of the agency and all members of staff. On Friday, Ella's account director on the retail fashion client had invited the whole team to her house for dinner. 'I've found a new recipe for Green Chicken Curry and I need guinea-pigs!'

Ella had gone into PR without knowing very much about it. She knew she was a good writer and she had always been interested in the news media ... PR looked like the kind of work which would use her talents and – maybe – offer a real career path. Within a month, she was certain she had made the right choice. She felt she was *lucky* to have hit on the right job at the right agency. At the same time, the founder of the agency felt she was lucky to have found Ella.

Working in PR is fast-paced. It can even be frenetic. It's an unusually collegiate environment. There's a feeling that 'you're all in it together' and you learn a lot from your senior colleagues. One thing that surprised me was how business-minded you need to be ... there's a lot of strategy involved, and the planning is very detailed. We have to align our work closely with the aims of the organization or client. Every initiative needs clear reasons, and we routinely analyse exactly why things worked (or not). It's important to be able to relate to senior people, which in some ways is a skill all of its own.

Ben Steele, Communications Officer at Sightsavers

No two days are the same – one day you might be securing an interview, the next managing a crisis or gaining media coverage for a key issue. But day-to-day, PR involves a lot of writing, media outreach and co-ordinating with teams to ensure consistent messaging. Building strong relationships, both with the media and within the organization or client, is crucial. You need resilience and you need to be adaptable – things can change quickly, and you often need to think on your feet.

Alexandra Bingham, Senior Media and Communications Officer, Mercy Corps

It's not easy to describe a typical day in PR – and that's the point! On any given day you're likely to receive a call from a journalist who needs a response within the hour, a critical question from a client about a recent piece of coverage, or notice of a potential crisis from the factory floor. You cannot expect to settle into routine in PR, and people starting their careers need to be able to thrive in changeable situations, taking time to relax when they can rather than when scheduled.

Oli Higgs, Senior PR Consultant with Speed Communications

There are many exceptions. If you are in the PR and communications department of a manufacturer of biosimilar pharmaceuticals, for example, your working life is likely to be more methodical and predictable than if you work in a business-to-consumer (B2C) PR agency (but no less challenging, stimulating and rewarding). If you work at a city agency handling a contested takeover you could find yourself putting in 18-hour shifts and sleeping at the office – the pressure is sometimes intense when everything's at stake for your client. If you work in entertainment PR, your hours will be the same as your clients' … you should be a night-owl. If you're in travel PR, you'll spend a lot of time away from home. If you work in food PR, your clients will pay attention if you like cooking, know a lot about ingredients, enjoy talking about implements and can quote the highest-profile celebrity chefs. If your clients sell derivatives, you need to know the difference between swaps and options. And so on.

Even so, PR and communications *does* have a distinct 'culture', style or atmosphere, and it's different from most other areas of professional business services. PR people are, in general, more friendly and sociable than the average person – this makes them very good colleagues, specially when you are young and new to the industry.

PR people have, in general, a creative outlook: they like to see things from a different angle, do things differently, come up with new and original ideas, be adventurous, try experimental approaches ... *anything* except 'going by the book'. This makes PR firms and departments stimulating places to work – as long as you like this kind of thing!

PR people, in general, are 'team players'. They enjoy working with other people more than working on their own. They get more of a buzz out of their group's success than from being singled out as a star. Their purpose is more to *assist* than to *score*. PR people are Reece James rather than Erling Haaland, Lauren Hemp rather than Lauren James.

PR people, in general, have chosen PR (or PR has chosen them) because they have a deep and genuine interest in other human beings. You don't get far in PR without a fairly high level of empathy. It's a *service business* ... what you're doing, day in and day out, is helping someone else to achieve *their* goals, *their* targets, *their* aspirations ... your clients may become rich and famous, but you yourself probably won't – and probably won't want to.

If you have talent and work hard, you'll make a good living. *Some* PR people make millions and even end up in the House of Lords – but if that's your goal in life, there are many better ways to achieve it than PR.

What's probable in PR and communications is that you'll be happier at work than many of your friends and many of your clients. That's a strong statement, I know. Where's the data? There isn't any that I know of – this is my *personal* opinion after years of working with thousands of PR people and thousands of people in other walks of life.

The Last Word

PR is exciting. You work with very senior people on very interesting challenges. No two days are the same. You work alongside all kinds of people – it's a big, diverse industry. There's not much routine. If you like talking to people – if you are sociable, or want to be ... if you're curious, thrive under pressure and want your work to be fun ... I can't think of a better career.

Rich Fogg, CEO of CCGroup

MINI-PRACTICAL

You have applied to a PR agency for a job as a trainee and you've been invited in for an interview. Here are some typical questions you could be asked. What would you say?

What do you think PR and communications is? How would you define it?

If you weren't thinking of PR, what other type of career would you have in mind?

Which headline story this morning caught your interest, and why?

Do you have favourite brands? Do you know why you are loyal to them?

Do any of your friends work in PR? If so, what have they told you about it?

What books are you reading at the moment?

Which are your favourite influencers, podcast hosts, YouTube stars?

If you could be Tolstoy or Richard Branson, which would you choose? Why?

A friend says: 'You've chosen PR? No! How could you?' What would you say?

A friend says: 'PR? Wow! Could you get me an interview?' What would you say?

What is the square root of 64?

What's the difference between a P&L and a balance sheet?

Which business tycoon has the best 'public image'? Which has the worst?

Do you know why HS2 has taken so long and cost so much?

Which three genres of music do you like best, and why?

Who is your favourite painter ever? Can you say why?

You have a spare hour this evening before going out to meet your friends. What will you watch, listen to or read? Or, if none of the above, what?

How will the Russia/Ukraine war end? How will the Israel/Palestine conflict end?

What was your favourite TV/streamed series this year? Why?

What is it about this agency/brand/company/charity that makes you want to work for us?

If we hire you, what do you expect to be doing in three years?

What is your ultimate goal in the PR and communications industry?

Why should you never say 'very unique' in media material?

It doesn't matter *what* you say as much as that you have *something* to say. Employers are looking for people who are curious, interested, well-informed and like to keep up with current affairs. The fragmentation of social media platforms, which many people – specially when they're young – depend on to the exclusion of all other sources, means they can end up with a fractional picture of what's really going on. This is no use in PR, where employers and clients depend on their PR advisors to know what *all* the media outlets are saying.

Employers will ask questions designed to give you an opportunity to tell them what you are really like. These are not 'trick questions' – the opposite. Employers know what kind of person will *probably* be happy and successful in their agency, team or department – and who *probably* won't. As you know, PR and communications is a career where success depends more on temperament, aptitude, talent and character than anything you could put on a spreadsheet. An interviewer's goal is to give you the best possible chance to tell her about yourself in 30 or 40 minutes. She will try her best to understand what makes you tick and what you've got to offer. The big question, when you're 20 years old, is your *potential*.

My own recommendation is for employers to spend *a lot of time* talking to potential employees. There aren't any short cuts. At least two conversations, ideally three, in different settings. If an employer is ready to invest time in talking to you, as a potential recruit, you know she is serious and you know she cares about giving you the best possible opportunity to show what you're like and what you will be able to contribute.

6

HOW TO CHOOSE YOUR
ENTRY-POINT

You've decided that public relations (PR) *could* be right for you and you *could* be right for PR. What now? We'll look later at apprenticeships, degree courses and what kinds of qualifications are most useful to someone considering a PR career. In this chapter, we'll talk about the factors which will guide your first steps into the industry – your first full-time, permanent job in PR and communications.

Question one: do you already have an intense interest in a particular area of commercial or cultural activity? For instance, you might be very interested in the computer industry ... or airlines ... or the design and construction of aircraft ... or fashion ... or cars ... or architecture ... or the movie industry ... or animal welfare... or healthcare, and so on.

If so, it makes sense to look for an opening in a company, or an agency, or an organisation which is wholly or mostly involved in that field of activity. If you can spend your working life absorbed in something you love – and get paid for it – you are half-way towards a happy and successful career.

A word of caution: it's probably obvious, but worth mentioning: areas that a lot of people are fascinated by - fashion, entertainment, art, travel and so on - are generally harder to get into and don't offer younger employees such good salaries and benefits as industries that are less sought-after. The jobs market really is a market. If people are queueing up, employers don't need to attract recruits with high salaries, so they don't.

The next point may be equally obvious, but could also be worth mentioning: if your top personal interest is of an 'academic' nature – archaeology, botany, Restoration Drama, Gregorian chants, marine invertebrates, the textile industry in 19th-century Manchester – it could be a good strategy to separate that interest from your career plans, at least if you are attracted to PR. You could be lucky and find a role in PR for the Great Egyptian Museum or the Helmshore Mills, but – as you'd expect – these opportunities are few and far between.

Question two: do you have a personal sense of mission? Do you want to spend your life making things better for other people, or animals, or certain kinds of people, or for certain countries, or the climate? Do you want to tackle the big problems afflicting the whole world, or issues affecting specific areas or groups? Do you strongly support a particular cause?

If so, you can (and possibly should) align your sense of purpose with your career by working – in PR and communications – for a charity or a philanthropic organisation. You will have seen that some of the contributors to this book have done exactly that. Charities need good exposure just as much as brands do – most depend on PR for donations, government support, putting their cause or issue onto the public debate agenda – and they value the skills of good communicators.

Question three: it's connected to the last question … do you feel more attracted by the private sector – companies, brands, business and commercial organisations – or by the public sector – government departments, local authorities, regulators, public bodies and institutions?

Here again, it's a decision that depends on how you *feel* you would like to spend your working life. Some people are naturally drawn to the 'cut-and-thrust' of the marketplace. Others feel more in tune with the idea of public service. There are fulfilling and rewarding roles for *persuasive communicators* in both areas.

It's worth mentioning here – and we'll say it again – that people can and do switch between private sector and public, commercial and philanthropic, national and international, business-to-consumer (B2C) and business-to-business (B2B) and corporate ... and back again ... at various points in the PR careers. You are never stuck in a particular niche – unless you want to be. Your PR skills are 'fungible'.

Question four: agency or in-house? Again, your initial preference doesn't have to be a permanent decision. People move all the time between agencies (consultancies) and in-house departments.

That said, the way you go about getting your first job is obviously different. So it makes sense and saves time to have *some* idea of where you think you would prefer to work.

PR agencies (consultancies, firms, companies, ...) range from small (up to 20 employees) through medium-sized to very large with hundreds of staff, specialised departments and teams and lots of offices. Each offers pluses and minuses to new recruits.

Small firms typically give new people more responsibility sooner. They tend to be less structured than larger firms and you are likely – as a new person – to have more direct, day-to-day contact with the founder or owner and other senior people. This usually means opportunities to learn quickly.

Medium-sized and larger firms have, as a rule, been around for longer (Edelman, for instance, was founded in 1952) which means they usually have specialist departments, just like other large organisations, to handle matters like human resources, information technology and accounts. In a smaller firm, these functions are quite likely to be managed personally by one or two of the directors.

If you prefer the idea of joining an in-house PR and communications team, the work you do will be broadly similar to what you'd be doing in an agency, but the environment will in most cases be much more structured and the pace is likely to be steadier. You will probably be working on a single programme, or brand, or campaign – at least in the beginning – which means you will have more time to learn about the products, brands, services ... in depth.

Question five: London or elsewhere? As mentioned earlier, London used to be *the* national centre of the media and communications industries – and to some extent that is still true. What's changed is that broadcasters and publishers today are just as likely to be found in Birmingham, Manchester Bristol, etc. The idea of 'Fleet Street' as an actual media hub, rather than a metonym, is long gone. Interestingly, the new media industries have reversed this trend: Meta, Apple and Alphabet all have large London offices. There are thriving new media clusters in Paddington, King's Cross and in the districts west, north and east of the City.

Social media, of course, can and does get produced anywhere its creators want to live and work. It could be Thailand or it could be Basingstoke.

For the PR and communications agency sector, what this means is that there are many firms based outside London with national and international clients … as well as many who have chosen to stick to the capital. The quality of work as between London and non-London is (*a personal view*) identical. Interesting clients are just as likely, these days, to retain an agency outside London.

What it means for you is that you can choose. Twenty years ago you might have felt that London offered unmissable career benefits … you might even have felt that it was 'London or nothing', in spite of the accommodation and cost-of-living issues. Today you can work and learn at a first-class PR firm almost anywhere you like. London might be on your future career radar … or it might not.

What matters most is that you begin your PR and communications career in a company or team where you feel that you fit. The most important element by far is the person you work for – 'your boss'. Will they take a personal interest in your progress? Will they have time to advise you, encourage you and give you feedback? Is this someone whose talents, skills and working style you admire? PR is not a theoretical or academic discipline – it's practical, all the way through – so the people you work for and learn from are extremely important factors in your personal progress.

PR agency or PR department? It really doesn't make any difference. Starting in-house may teach you how organisations really work, and this knowledge can be very valuable whether you are working in-house or in a consultancy later on. One of the many good things about PR is that you always have a choice.

Luke Blair, Director of Communications at an NHS hospital group

HOW FAST WILL YOU PROGRESS?

You should expect to spend a year, or maybe two, 'learning the ropes' as a *trainee* – though you might be called a junior executive, an assistant executive or any one of a number of other designations. Your next step is to become an Account Executive – the first rung on the career advancement ladder (in most agencies – terminology can differ).

After another two years, or maybe three, you should aim to become an Account Manager. This is a big step because you'll need to acquire a number of new skills – planning and controlling budgets, client relationship management, taking responsibility for junior colleagues' performance and progress – as well as continuing to demonstrate excellent content production and stakeholder engagement ability.

Three or four years later, you will be ready to become an Account Director. This means you will be in charge of a team of people and a group of clients, working under the (light) supervision of a senior person, but very much in charge of the show. If you have what it takes as an Account Director – not just competence but also ambition and a willingness to 'go the extra mile' – you can expect to be invited, sooner or later, to become an Associate Director. This is the ante-room to the board itself.

But we are looking many years ahead. The best advice for now is to expect to spend between one and three years climbing each of these rungs on the ladder.

WHAT IF YOU FEEL YOU DON'T FIT?

After three months or six months, you may feel you have made the wrong choice. This happens to quite a lot of people, and it's usually because their relationship with their manager isn't working out as they had hoped.

The great thing about PR and communications is that it doesn't matter very much. PR is possibly the most mobile professional business service. We can switch and switch back – from private to public sector, from B2C to B2B, from national to international, from aviation to financial derivatives to production automation, from food to cosmetics to movies, from Glasgow to Munich to Marlow – without much difficulty.

There is a basic set of skills you possess and develop in your career as a *persuasive communicator*. Within reason, it matters less how much you know than how well you can apply these skills to the marketing or issues-management challenge in front of you.

WHAT KIND OF CURRICULUM VITAE WILL CONVINCE EMPLOYERS TO SEE YOU?

Everyone reading this book will know how to use artificial intelligence (AI) to construct a perfect curriculum vitae (CV).

Here are some tips anyway.

Make It Short

Everyone in any kind of organisation feels that they are under pressure, short of time. In PR and communications, this is very likely to be true. Brevity is the key requirement of successful media material. Demonstrate it in your resume.

What I look for in new recruits is writing ability, curiosity and emotional intelligence. An ex-journalist with good people-skills is ideal. You can make a judgement about how well they can write and whether or not they are curious about the world around them from a CV, but emotional intelligence can only be assessed from a face-to-face meeting.

Euan Edworthy, MBE, Senior Partner at Best Communications

Catch Their Interest – Be Surprising

Most CVs (bios and resumes) are somewhat cookie-cutter. *Take a bow, AI.* Good media material attracts the reader's interest with something surprising ... show you can do this in your CV.

For instance, when did you first realise that the pen is mightier than the sword? How and why? What did Ivy Lee say that made you think PR could be the career for you? Did you escape death by inches when a shark attacked your sub-aqua group in the Red Sea? How did you feel when you reached the summit of Mont Blanc at sunrise? What was the best career advice you ever heard, and who from? And so on.

We want people who stand out, who are unafraid to make a point or put forward an idea. We look for natural enthusiasm – without a whiff of arrogance. People who can structure their thinking, particularly when asked for their view of a particular problem or their ideas for solutions. People who can explain their own thought-processes.

And, fundamentally, people you *know* clients and teammates are going to enjoy being around.

Dominic Church, Senior Partner at WA Communications

Make It Personal

Employers are used to being approached on a mass basis by young people looking for a job. It's similar to journalists receiving a press release sent to 60 other reporters. They don't like it very much, and nor would you.

'I want to work for Phenomenal PR because ....'

If you know something about the firm you are applying to – and, of course, you do – tell them why *their* firm is the PR agency or PR department of your dreams. Don't worry about 'flattery' – they'll know what you're doing, but they'll appreciate it anyway.

What's Special About You?

Imagine that 50 people are sending their CVs to the person in charge of the agency or department that you'd like to join as a trainee. PR and communications is a growing sector, but the creative industries are a popular choice.

You need to *stand out from the crowd*. You'll need to stand out from the crowd – exactly the same thing – when you start work in PR. Only one story in a hundred gets covered by valuable outlets.

Show you can do it in your bio!

Presentation and Delivery

Use video if you think your screen presence is compelling, but make it an option.

Delivery … this may seem quaint by the time this book is published … but have you considered going retro and sending your CV round by hand, on paper, in an envelope? When everything is digital – convenient and handy, but never exactly loveable – stepping out of line by using the old methods could be a stand-out factor.

Unless, by the time this is published, everyone's doing it.

Include a Picture

You might hate the idea. However, something like 80 per cent of the memorable impact of a person trying to sell something to someone else depends on their appearance. Not the facts, not the words. What they look like, their expressions, gestures, etc.

Maximise your chances by getting some good pictures taken. A point about professional photographers … they know techniques that the rest of us don't, even though we all take pictures and we can all do image enhancement. Are there any photography or cinematography students among your friends?

PREVIOUS EXPERIENCE COUNTS FOR A LOT

Imagine yourself as a PR agency or department head, looking for new people who will fit in, revel in their role and become successful. What signals would *you* look for?

You know that writing ability, curiosity about current affairs and 'people skills' are the most important factors employers want. If you are young, you might not think you have very much previous experience to cite.

But you probably have more than you imagine ... temporary or part-time jobs while you were at school or as a student ... things you learnt when travelling in a gap-year or during vacations ... writing you may have done as an online contributor ... working on the college 'newspaper' ... parts you may have played in student dramatic productions ... ability you may have as a musician ... events you may have played a role in organising, etc.

All these experiences, at school or college or university, or in the spaces in between, could be very relevant to your future PR career, and - if so - should be highlighted in your CV.

Imagine an employer who needs a new recruit, looking at 20 CVs. What will catch her attention and make that CV stand out from the other 19? If you can think like this, and do it, you are proving right away that you are – probably – a natural PR person.

MINI-PRACTICAL

Imagine you work for a petfood company – WAGS! – or at the agency looking after their PR.

WAGS! is a challenger brand, competing for shelf-space and media attention with much larger, better-established rivals. Their products are good quality and well-priced, but WAGS! doesn't automatically get much coverage in the media. They depend on creative PR solutions from the people in our team.

We want to send the message that people who **really** love their dogs will give them WAGS!

Can you think of an opinion-survey among dog-owners that reinforces the idea that dogs are people's best friends? Can you think of an image-based campaign on social media that associates the WAGS! brand with an idyllic dog/human relationship? How about a range of WAGS!-branded merchandise ...? What comes to mind?

You'll need to find new, unique and engaging angles to make the headlines.

I interviewed dozens, if not hundreds, of people at MSL. Curiosity is the first requirement. Writing ability – I think that's obvious. Then it's probably an eye for detail. I remember one candidate who really made a strong impression. It was a young man who'd been working in a small agency outside London. We were knocked out: he was obviously mature, though young; clever, but with a gentle manner; charming and fun. He looked you straight in the eye and genuinely listened – though he also had lots to say for himself. He was the only person we ever created a vacancy for. He's now head of corporate for a major multinational.

My personal favourite is detail. Without it, everything else falls apart. But many would disagree.

Jackie Elliot, Chair of Cathcart Consulting and a
Former Chair of the PRCA

7

DO YOU NEED QUALIFICATIONS
OR A DEGREE?

A degree is not essential for a career in public relations and communications – you can sign up for an apprenticeship instead, or switch to PR from a different career altogether – but, if you like the idea of studying for three years, a degree is a useful asset. Most of the people I've talked to give the same advice: 'If you want to go to university, do it. But do it for its own sake, not because you think you need a degree to work in public relations'.

What kind of degree is useful in a PR career? The answer is: almost any. If you're attracted by PR at an early age, there are PR modules at many UK universities, very often as components of degree courses in marketing communications and/or media studies. There are also BA (Hons) courses in PR itself, for example, at the University of the Arts in London.

My personal opinion is that almost any arts or humanities degree will enhance your skills in researching and marshalling facts, analysing information, making rational judgements and expressing your conclusions cogently – all of which is vital if you work in PR. The actual subject you study is *almost* irrelevant – it's the thinking and writing experience that's valuable.

If you are studying a STEM subject, you are probably thinking of a different career. But who knows? Mark Adams studied physics, went into PR and became a PR superstar. My quantum mechanics colleague was a gifted mathematician and could have worked at a research institute or a hedge-fund, but chose PR consultancy instead. The realm of *science communication* can be very rewarding for people with the ability to master a scientific subject and who also have a talent for writing and speaking.

> I always loved reading and writing and I studied literature at university. When I graduated I looked for a job involving writing. I worked for a while as a freelance journalist, but what I really liked was working as part of a team. Public relations was the answer.
>
> *Ben Steele, Communications Officer at Sightsavers*
>
> I knew the kind of thing I wanted to do by the time I took A-levels. I was good at English, so I was thinking about the media ... advertising ... public relations? Then I heard a talk from a PR expert at Bournemouth University and that helped me make up my mind.
>
> I don't think it matters what type of degree you have. Some of the most talented people I've met in PR have all kinds of degrees. It's much more about curiosity, a love of reading and writing, social interaction ... aptitudes. Though I'd say that a good command of English is essential.
>
> *Rich Fogg, CEO of CCGroup*
>
> There is no single path into public relations. You can enter the industry from school, from university or 'sideways' from something else. I think it's true that graduates usually know something about PR as a career option but school-leavers very often don't. Yet there are many opportunities for young people – they know how to communicate with young target audiences much better than colleagues who are only five or six years older.
>
> University isn't for everyone. Apprenticeships offer a very good alternative. When I'm asked I usually say: if you don't feel you *really* want to go to university, don't. You can always study for a degree later on if you change your mind.

> If you're at school, your future job probably doesn't exist yet! Things change fast in the communications industry. If you're at university ... do you like to keep up with the news? If so, public relations could be exactly right for you.
>
> *Ann-Marie Blake is a well-known consultant, advisor and educator in communications*

Do employers place importance on degrees? They vary. Some consider a degree as a kind of threshold; others think real-world experience is more valuable; others, specially these days, like the idea of recruiting school-leavers – perhaps into an apprenticeship scheme – and providing on-the-job training.

Graduate or not, you'll receive the training and coaching you need once you've started work. Some of this is, of course, informal – watching how your senior colleagues do things, getting feedback, improving week by week. But much of it is more formal. All large agencies and many small firms operate some kind of training system or 'Academy' for employees right up to the level of account director. They send people away on courses to acquire various management skills. Many agencies and many in-house departments sign their people up for courses with Public Relations and Communications Association (PRCA) training – either classroom sessions or online – and encourage them to acquire PRCA qualifications.

As you'd expect, large organisations nearly all have well-organised training and Continuing Professional Development (CPD) programmes for all staff, including their PR and communications specialists. Communicators in government departments, for example, receive excellent training and CPD under the auspices of the Government Communications Service.

ALTERNATIVE TYPES OF USEFUL EXPERIENCE

Some people, like myself or Ben Steele, got their start in PR after working in the media. People like Luke Blair move into PR after successful careers as well-known journalists or correspondents.

You will meet a lot of ex-journalists in PR agencies and departments. This is because, as we've already discussed, writing is the core PR skill and accounts for about 60 per cent of how PR people spend their time at work.

Any kind of writing job will be valuable experience, whether you go into PR from school or from university.

Get real-world experience – almost any kind of work is useful – retail, travel ... meet different kinds of people, learn how they think and what their interests are ... don't worry yet about your career ... discover what you like and don't like. If you're at college or university you may be able to land a temporary job in public relations, but almost anything will fill out your knowledge of the world and help you decide what kind of industry will appeal to you when it comes to finding a public relations role in an agency or a department.

Richard Bailey is an editor, PR educator and former
university lecturer

If you're a student considering PR, gaining hands-on experience through internships or placements can be invaluable for getting a foot in the door.

Alexandra Bingham, Senior Media and Communications
Officer at Mercy Corps

Think about the skills you have, or can acquire while you're studying, which would be useful in a PR career – *transferrable skills*. I know from my own experience you'll have some. For example, studying political communications at uni taught me the basics of planning a media campaign. Growing up in a TV newsroom gave me an insight into writing news stories. Working in a four-star hotel gave me experience of managing clients and making sales calls. I didn't know it at the time, but these were great *transferrable skills* for a career in PR. What are yours?

Stuart McBride is head of PR for a financial
trade association

Don't overthink it! There are so many skills and qualities needed for a role in PR. Taking an interest in current
affairs ... having the ability to research and analyse something critically ... understanding how people engage and
communicate with each other in today's digital age – it's all
useful. Whatever your background you'll be able to align
your skills and experience with what the industry needs.

Itty Elora, Talent Manager (PR, Comms and Advertising)
at the Advertising Association

What's a good degree for a career in PR and communications? You don't have to specialize yet. I think the best education for PR is a well-rounded one. Keep your interests
broad and learn about life. Any degree is relevant – though
maybe courses that lean on writing skills are a little more
so. PR is not a job for theorists, it's a job for practitioners –
so you'll learn everything you need to know about public
relations once you start work. Whether you're at school or
university, or in between, the main thing is to develop people skills and the ability to organize. The best degree for
someone who wants to succeed in PR is the one that interests you most.

Luke Blair, Director of Communications at an NHS
hospital group

When exploring a career in PR, it's worth noting that the
industry favours either relevant work experience *or* formal
training. When thinking about experience, don't just limit
yourself to PR! Any role that you can justify as helping to
develop your skills in communication, creativity, customer
relations or analytical thinking can help you stand out. For
example, a role in retail or hospitality might initially fit the
bill. Now link that experience to your personal interests or
hobbies ... do you write a blog, have you organized events,
how engaged are you with the media? When writing an
application/cover letter, think also about what you have taken
ownership of and the impact you've made on the teams
you've worked in.

Aside from the key PR skills, companies want to know that you have a genuine interest and a willingness to collaborate. Realistically, everything else can be taught!

There is also some truth to the saying: 'Your network is your net worth'. Think about how you can meet PR professionals and be inquisitive while you're at it. You could start by contacting agencies in your local area for internship opportunities, or joining a membership body to meet like-minded professionals and potential future employers at events.

Stephanie Umebuani, former Head of Apprenticeships at the PRCA

APPRENTICESHIPS IN PR

Apprenticeships are a clever way of combining working with studying under the aegis of the Department for Education's apprenticeship scheme. There are four levels and completing an apprenticeship can take between one and five years.

A number of large organisations offer apprenticeships in PR and communications, as do some agencies and consultancies. The PRCA is very active in encouraging, organising and helping to manage apprenticeships in PR and communications, so if you are interested in PR but not interested in a university degree course, the PRCA would be a good place to begin your enquiry.

THE PROFESSIONAL BODIES

The UK PR industry has two professional bodies. Their purpose is to maintain and develop the highest standards of professional conduct, integrity and ethics in the practice of PR, while at the same time providing training and qualifications, conferences and events for both specialist and general-practice members. Both bodies operate award schemes to encourage creativity and effectiveness in their members' work, and both have an international dimension.

The PRCA enforces professional conduct by means of its Standards Committee, which reviews and publishes the PRCA's Code of Conduct and investigates possible infractions. The Chartered Institute of Public Relations does the equivalent via its Professional Practices Committee.

Members comprise agencies, in-house departments and individuals. If you are considering a career in PR, it would be a good idea to join, attend meetings (which are held all over the country) and find out about the opportunities for training, qualifications, certificates and diplomas on offer.

The wonderful thing about a PR career is that while it can, of course, be built on an academic foundation it can also be successfully built on a practical basis. PR offers the opportunity to learn new skills and hone them literally from Day One of working in an agency or an in-house department. The operational side of the job is very much practical and you can personally make an impact on an organization or a client very early on. The sheer variety of work always keeps things interesting and the pace of life in an agency or in-house department keeps you sharp, too. In terms of careers, it's one of the most rewarding around.

Steve Dunne, CEO of Digital Drums and a renowned PR trainer

SPECIALIST AREAS OF PR AND COMMUNICATIONS

Healthcare communications: as noted earlier, if you are drawn to PR work in the pharmaceutical industry, you may have been interested in the medical or biological sciences for years already. It is relatively unusual for PR people with an arts or marketing background to transition into the highly specialised, highly regulated world of healthcare communications (although it does happen).

Over-the-counter pharmaceuticals (painkillers, vitamins, cold-relief and the like) are sold in a similar way to any other branded product, but *ethical* pharmaceuticals are very different. They must be prescribed by a medical practitioner in a surgery, clinic or hospital. There are strict rules controlling how PR and communications

for these treatments may be conducted – not only government regulations but also rules set by self-regulatory bodies like the Association of the British Pharmaceutical Industry (ABPI) and (European
Federation of Pharmaceutical Industries and Associations (EFPIA)
If you work in this area you not only need to know a lot about the
science but you also need to be very familiar with the rules and
codes governing PR and communications.

Large PR agencies are likely to have specialist healthcare divi-
sions. There are numerous smaller consultancies who do healthcare
and nothing else. Then there are the pharma companies themselves
and the whole infrastructure of UK healthcare, including – of
course – the NHS itself, but also including research laboratories,
health-related charities and the many institutions and associations
focussed on different specialisations.

Investor relations: sometimes referred to as 'City PR' or financial
communications, this specialist area is also strictly regulated. If your
work entails communicating with investors and the people who
influence their decisions, you need to know the Stock Exchange
rules inside-out, as well as those regulations set by bodies like the
Financial Conduct Authority (FCA). This sector also has a specialist
industry association, the Investor Relations Society, which exists to
encourage best practice in much the same way as the PRCA.

Financial communications is exciting, demanding and rewarding. Your work is involved with helping companies raise funds, go
public – probably through an initial public offering (IPO) – negoti-
ate mergers, make acquisitions, fight off unwelcome acquirers, etc.
If the world of bids and deals interests you, this could be the right
choice. Financial communications is dominated by specialist agencies, some of them very large, though some general practice consultancies also provide financial communications as part of their
corporate communications services.

Is financial communications a separate world? Some say so – it's
a relatively small community, with a limited number of decision-
makers and opinion-formers. Networking is at a premium. There's
often a great deal of money at stake, so the pressure can be intense.
On the other hand, the key skill is *persuasive communications*.
Most of the major City PR firms belong to the PRCA.

Public affairs, also known as government relations and
'lobbying', is the third specialist area which is subject not only to

the PRCA's regulatory processes but also to its own registration system. Like financial communications, public affairs is in some ways a separate world.

According to Lionel Zetter, author of *Lobbying – The Art of Political Persuasion*, the first requirement for a successful career in public affairs is an intense personal interest in politics. 'You have to be absolutely fascinated by the whole subject.' You need to be a very good listener: 'Political people love to talk!' and adept at forging and maintaining personal relationships. Other key skills are similar to the requirements in other varieties of PR: 'Writing ability, analytical thinking, a strong interest in current affairs and an insatiable appetite for political news and commentary'.

Most people aiming for a public affairs career will have a degree, and perhaps also a post-graduate degree, in politics. They have probably worked in student politics and may have volunteered on an MP's campaign or become actively involved in politics at a local level. Their first full-time job could be in a public affairs consultancy – where they might have completed an internship – or it could be on an MP's staff as a researcher, a case-worker.

It would be fair to say that the world of public affairs is much more about the world of politics than about the world of PR. Some public affairs consultants become MPs and Special Advisors, while some MPs and ministers later join the public affairs community. It's not a professional area that people end up in by chance – so, if public affairs is your goal, you almost certainly already know it.

Once you've got an idea which industry sector attracts you, or which area of public relations, it's time to start looking for a job. The PRCA website lists apprenticeship vacancies, routes into PR and the skills employers look for – that's an excellent starting-point. As well as that, websites like Indeed. co.uk and Reed.co.uk list a lot of vacancies – and a growing number of firms are recruiting through LinkedIn, so you might like to create an account and start looking on there.

Stuart McBride is head of PR at a financial trade association

I 'studied' history and politics at university. I didn't learn a lot that I couldn't have learnt some other way. Did I enjoy it, make new friends and grow as a person? Yes. Did it make any difference to my career? Not really ... though years later I found myself at a dinner with nine other senior PR people. It turned out that we'd all studied history in some form. This doesn't prove anything except, perhaps, that an interest in history is a good foundation for a career in public relations.

I think it's true that PR offers a lot to the many thousands of people who have studied for non-vocational degrees and are not certain what they want to do with their lives.

What about PR degrees – which I taught for over a decade? The (limited) evidence is that people with PR degrees are likely to be serious about a life-long career in PR, which is a factor employers rather like. But there is no evidence that people with PR degrees are better at PR, or more highly sought-after, than people with degrees in something else. My advice: do a degree in a subject you find interesting, at a university with a good social life.

Or forget about doing a degree and do an apprenticeship instead. I was a sceptic when PR apprenticeships first started, but I've been converted by the calibre and drive of the people who've taken them up. An apprenticeship also means, of course, that you are free of a mountain of student debt. Whatever the reason, the apprentices I've met are terrifically upbeat and positive.

Trevor Morris is a best-selling PR author and the former
CEO of Chime PR

What Do You Learn on a PR Degree Course?

The university PR degree landscape changes year by year, but as a rule of thumb, the larger universities offer PR as a sub-set of a broader course in communications, media or marketing, while some smaller colleges offer courses entirely devoted to PR. As our contributors have said several times in this book, PR is not an academic subject – so it could make sense to opt for a course which combines PR with other cognate subjects that will be valuable in a communications career – whether or not you specialise in PR per se once you start work.

What topics might you find on these courses? Media relations, community relations and corporate social responsibility (CSR), internal (employee) relations, issues and crisis management, investor relations, consumer relations, PR ethics, PR in its political and socio-economic context, writing skills, critical thinking, personal skills such as time management, social media proficiency, digital marketing competence ... together with the history and development of PR as a specialised professional business service. Most courses aim to combine the background theory with a strong emphasis on practical skills, hands-on experience and understanding the media's role in shaping public opinion.

MINI-PRACTICAL

One of the big banks has briefed us to launch a new pension product for them. When we asked what was special about it, they told us it was a fairly standard scheme, more or less the same as everything else offered by the large and well-known financial services companies. We guessed that they would rely on their branches, advisors and direct contact with customers to reach their sales targets.

But what about PR? How can we interest the media in a financial product which, in the client's own words, is very similar to everything else on the market?

How would you use your imagination to create a successful media story about a product that has nothing new or different to say? Could you embed the launch of the new pension in a story which *does* have something interesting to offer potential customers? Can you 'package' the news of the pension launch inside more engaging media content?

8

EARLY DAYS – HOW TO SHINE

Let's imagine you've got an internship in a public relations agency or department, or you've landed a PR role – temporary or part-time – with a charity or a local organisation. This might be your first job in an office or a team. You want to stand out. Here are some tips.

Think about how to make a good personal impression. This means 'looking the part'. If you've already been to the office for an interview, you'll know the 'dress code' – everywhere has one, even if it's not written down. If you don't know, phone up and ask.

Be bright and cheerful – a radiator. Even if you're feeling nervous, confused or in low spirits – don't let it show. Instead, try to be the person who puts a smile on people's faces when you come into the room. This is a good strategy in any job, anywhere – but it's specially important in PR, where positivity and optimism are the keynotes.

Be a sponge. We talked earlier about the importance of being a 'good listener'. Not only is this by far the best way to learn, it's also the best way to make other people enjoy your company. There's an old saying: *you have two ears and one mouth – use them in that ratio.*

Punctuality matters. If you're late, you're probably keeping someone waiting, which means you're wasting their time. A good rule is to always be five minutes early.

Make it obvious that you're eager to learn. Most people in PR know useful methods and techniques that you won't find in books, and senior people know a lot of these. Most people in PR love sharing their knowledge with younger colleagues – PR people are nearly all helpful by nature. If you're keen to learn, your colleagues will be a gold-mine.

Start networking right away. This is what Rich Fogg called 'social dexterity'. Show a *genuine* interest in your colleagues as people. Remember their names and what they tell you about themselves. Some people can do this without effort, but, if not, the effort is worth making. Networking skill is central to the practice of PR and essential for a successful PR career.

Show that you're a good team player. Is one of your colleagues snowed under, having difficulty? Can you give them a hand? Good team players set aside their own priorities to help other members of the team. When everyone does this, the team becomes much more effective and the work is much more fun.

Be rock-solid reliable. Make a point of delivering exactly what you promised, exactly when you promised it (or earlier). This is Rule One for developing good media relationships – and it also, for obvious reasons, makes you a valued colleague in your new team.

Never delay email or phone responses. You know what it's like when you're waiting, waiting for a reply … annoying, maybe frustrating … not helpful. Be the person who makes everyone else's lives easier by answering at once (or, if you can't, as soon as possible). *When I worked for WPP, I was in charge of a very small fragment of Martin Sorrell's global empire. But I could expect a reply to an email within 24 hours, and usually 12, at any time of day or night, wherever he was in the world.*

Learn the language quickly. Every profession, trade, company and department has its own jargon – some of it professional terminology, some of it just the lingo that has evolved in that group. Every team has its own 'form-and-fit' – its own preferred way of doing things (like how long meetings last, how documents should be presented and so on). Get to know these things, large and small, as fast as you can.

Be ready to socialise. PR is a very 'sociable' profession, so it's quite likely that your colleagues will ask you to join them for coffee, lunch, drinks after work ... be prepared to spend personal time in your colleagues' company (within reason).

IN PR, YOUR WRITTEN WORK IS ALL-IMPORTANT

Copy, stories, content, compositions, prose, whatever you call it, the quality of your written work is the hallmark of someone who is valued by their team from Day One and is all set for a successful career in PR. Our tip: take exaggerated care over the presentation, accuracy and structure of your written work.

Brevity. Journalists train for years learning how to compress their stories into as few words as possible. Sub-editors exist to cut reporters' copy and make it more concise. Succinct writing is *far* more effective ... but no-one teaches us how to do it at school or college. We have to teach ourselves. As a rule of thumb, cut whatever you've drafted by 20 per cent.

Structure. Short sentences (20 words) and short paragraphs (two or three sentences). Much easier to read ... much more persuasive. Short words, too ... use plain, everyday language whenever you can.

Accuracy. Never send anything to anyone without pausing, doing something else, then coming back to see if you can improve it. You always can. Proofing: change the font and print your copy out. You'll spot things on paper that you won't notice on the screen. Then read it backwards. Read it out loud (in the right direction) – you'll *hear* ways to improve your writing that won't be obvious when you're reading it. Finally, ask a colleague to give you constructive criticism before you send your document off.

DIGITAL EXPERTISE AND ARTIFICIAL INTELLIGENCE

As you know, online channels, platforms and services are at least as important for engaging with your audiences as mainstream media, events, direct contact and *ambient media* or *exposure marketing*. Are you the most knowledgeable social media expert in your circle? You probably are, but if not – with a PR career in mind – you probably should be.

Advertising and PR have never been as distinct as some people said, and nowadays the differences are paper-thin. When it comes to influencers, there's no difference at all. It pays for us – PR people – to give close attention to how advertising agencies are evolving in their use of online/digital ... some of the most imaginative, creative minds in commercial communications are to be found in advertising agencies ... what can we learn from them?

Artificial Intelligence (AI - Large Language Models, or LLMs, like ChatGPT) has changed the way some agencies and PR people produce their work already, and will unquestionably affect the way we *all* work in coming years. AI can save time by producing copy from our briefs, leaving us the shorter task of editing, polishing and tidying up an AI draft. AI can help us with planning and collecting data for tasks like audience and stakeholder analysis. It hasn't yet replaced the need for human creativity – though it might, who knows? There are still nuances of expression that LLMs can't master – or haven't yet.

If you are intent on a career in PR, or in the early stages of gathering experience in PR and communications, it's a good idea to experiment with AI – for fun, if not at work – and see what it can do for *you* ... how it can save you time, how it can help you make sure that your plans and schedules leave nothing out, how it can provoke or inspire creative thinking, how it can instantly assemble the facts and figures that you need for your document ... but, if you are planning a career in PR, you are probably already an expert user of AI.

ARE YOU AN EXPERT ON SOMETHING? COULD YOU BE?

It's often said that the ideal member of a PR team is a 'T-shaped' person, meaning that they have a broad range of skills and knowledge across the map, but are also unusually knowledgeable or adept in one or two particular areas of expertise. This makes them a 'go-to' person for their team colleagues as well as a valuable asset for certain kinds of client advisory work.

It doesn't really matter what these areas of expertise are, as long as they have some potential application to the communications work we are going to be doing for our future clients or employers. Knowing all about the design of ancient Greek triremes probably doesn't qualify, but having in-depth knowledge of local politics certainly could, or knowing all there is to know about the airline industry, or the TV industry, or movie production. Best of all, perhaps, would be to arrive at your first job as a fully-fledged expert in infographics, broadcast-quality video production… or whatever other new communications art or science is capturing the industry's interest when you are looking for your first position.

'BE THERE OR BE SQUARE'

A lot of PR work can be accomplished screen-to-screen. A lot of communication, in groups or person-to-person, can be conducted on Zoom, Teams and the like, with considerable economies of time and money. During lockdown, we didn't have much choice, and today most PR people spend at least some of their time working from home.

However, the really important results in PR (and any other kind of professional services industry) emerge from physical, face-to-face contact. There is no substitute: this is the only way to initiate, build, develop and maintain the relationships with clients, colleagues, media, influencers and stakeholders on which great PR work depends.

Our recommendation: get out there, speak up, take part … meet your clients and connections 'in real life' … take every opportunity you can to forge new friendships, exchange information and opinions, make a good personal impression, become 'part of the scene' – or many different scenes – and make your mark.

MINI-PRACTICAL

We have a problem on our hands. The client is a new budget airline offering a stripped-down service to destinations where demand is still ahead of capacity. We were briefed to turn the inaugural flight from Luton to Bratislava into a major media event. Our team did well: TV was there, the Mayor was ready to greet the first passengers with a bouquet, a Slovak brass band was waiting on the tarmac and 20 students in national costume were ready on the red carpet to hand out local specialties as everyone disembarked.

The plane didn't arrive on time. After 30 minutes, there was still no sign. After an hour, the Mayor had to leave, the brass band packed up their instruments and the students went back to the city. The media wanted to know what had happened, but we had to say we didn't know. But we did know: the client had given us the wrong date.

How can we recover credibility with the media and other stakeholders?

The best people I met in PR were engaging, warm and sometimes bold. If they were also genuinely funny or strongly creative, that was a real find. They were always good or great writers who had the fundamentals of writing – grammar, spelling and punctuation – nailed. They were confident and self-assured but also emotionally intelligent: an advisor must have an opinion and express it without coming across as arrogant, while also listening for the client's reactions and changing tack in a moment to find different ways to persuade. The best PR people were articulate and – even better – eloquent. They were clever, strategic thinkers with a quick-witted intelligence that was worldly rather than purely academic. They were brilliant inter-personally and always courteous. You had a strong sense that, with colleagues and clients who shared those qualities, they would build real and lasting friendships.

*Jan Stannard started as an office junior and
ultimately established her own consultancy.
She is the Co-founder of Heal Rewilding.*

Jan asked ChatGPT if it agreed with her. It did. Here's what it said:

Exceptional PR professionals possess a blend of interpersonal, strategic and creative qualities that enable them to build and maintain strong relationships while effectively communicating messages. Some key qualities:

Strategic thinking: they see the bigger picture and align communication strategies with organizational goals, anticipating challenges and opportunities.

Exceptional communication skills: they write and speak with clarity, precision and adaptability, tailoring messages to different audiences and platforms.

Relationship building: they excel at cultivating strong, trusting relationships with clients, media, stakeholders and internal teams.

Emotional intelligence: they demonstrate empathy, tact and an ability to read people and situations, which helps in managing relationships and challenges effectively.

Creativity: they think 'outside the box' generating innovative ideas for campaigns, story-telling and problem-solving.

Resilience: they stay calm and effective under pressure, handling crises or setbacks with professionalism and focus.

Adaptability: they can pivot strategies quickly in response to changing circumstances, trends or audience needs.

Media savvy: they understand how the media operates and know how to craft compelling stories that resonate with journalists and audiences alike.

Persuasiveness: they can influence opinions and gain buy-in from diverse groups.

Attention to detail: they ensure all messaging is polished, accurate and aligned with the brand voice.

Strong networking skills: they maintain a robust network of media contacts, influencers and industry professionals, using these connections to amplify their campaigns.

Analytical thinking: they measure the impact of their campaigns using data and then adjust strategies to achieve optimal results.

Integrity: they maintain honesty and ethical standards of conduct.

An exceptional PR professional combines these qualities with a passion for storytelling and an instinct for managing perceptions and reputations.

9

DEVELOPING YOUR PERSONAL BRAND

Once you start work, you'll want to make your career accelerate as fast as possible by 'making a name for yourself'. With any luck this will happen anyway – you're keen, you're competent, you have writing and creative talent, you're a good team-member – but, even so, there are steps you can take to push things along. What this entails (this may sound odd) is *doing public relations for yourself.*

Why not start now, while you're still at school or university, or in-between?

GET TO KNOW YOUR LOCAL MEDIA – PERSONALLY

Ask the editors of your local titles if they could spare you half-an-hour – because you are trying to learn as much as possible about the media industry. You can also try this if there are local or regional TV/radio stations within reach. Have a list of good questions before you arrive – editors and journalists love telling people things, so you'll learn a lot. Don't be shy – the media make their living by demanding other people's time, so they'll be amused, and even impressed, if you ask for theirs.

Is there a local journalist or broadcaster whose work you admire? Write and ask if she or he could spare you 30 minutes to find out what being a journalist is really like – are PR people helpful, and what are their tips on being a PR person who their media contacts truly value? I have done this all my life when starting work on clients in unfamiliar industries, and I can promise that – if the journalist believes you're sincere – they will always find time for you.

You might even wangle an invitation to write something for one of these outlets – 'how young people see their prospects in the local labour market' (or whatever). Any future employer would be highly impressed to see that you have already been published.

ARE THERE LOCAL ASSOCIATIONS OR ACTION-GROUPS THAT YOU COULD JOIN?

There are probably lots of business groups in your local area. The Chamber of Commerce, of course, but many more. Could you join one of them and volunteer your services in a PR or communications capacity? The same thing goes for action-groups, which are usually all about PR and communications. Are there any that you personally support, where you could lend a hand and, at the same time, garner valuable experience – plus something extra to put on your CV?

If you already have an active interest in a local activity – drama, perhaps, a sports team, a local festival – could you offer your services in a PR and communications role for them?

HOW ABOUT LOCAL COMPANIES?

Are there companies nearby with PR departments where you would be welcome as an 'observer' – somewhere between 'fly on the wall' and *work shadowing*? It could be worth asking. Are there PR agencies in your locality who – even if they can't offer internships – would be happy to have you around to watch what people do and ask questions? The answer is probably 'yes' if you just ask.

As we've noted before, PR people are by nature helpful and – in my experience – kind-hearted. If they can do something to help a young person find out about their industry, they probably will.

YOUR PERSONAL FAMILY/FRIENDS/
NEIGHBOURS NETWORK

We're not suggesting that you're a nepo-baby! There aren't many in PR, and if you were one of them you wouldn't be reading this book.

However, have you thought systematically about the connections that your wider family has, and the connections that those connections have at their disposal? Could any of them help you get some kind of experience – an internship ideally, but – if not – just an opportunity to look and learn – at a company, a media outlet and an agency?

Likewise with your own friends and friends of family members. Had you forgotten that Ria's dad is head of marketing at Lancashire E-Vehicles? Now you think about it … *of course!* David's uncle is features editor of the East Midlands News Group. And – *duh!* – your tennis partner's mum is a presenter at South-West TV.

We don't think about these links when we're at school. Why should we? They're not relevant. But now they are.

YOUR OWN BLOG?

Could you set up and run your own blog about something that interests you passionately? If not that, could you be a frequent contributor to other people's blogs, vlogs and podcasts? If not that, could you say what you think on discussion threads?

The idea here is to get early experience in what it's like to find out about a topic, think about it, compose an interesting item about it – and get it published. I've met some enterprising PR people who did exactly this when they were still at school or university, and I've never met a single one who regretted it.

HOW ABOUT HELPING TO MARKET
A SCHOOL OR UNIVERSITY EVENT?

Most schools, colleges and universities will 'bite your arm off' if you offer to help in any capacity with organising an event.

But you're a bit different – you've decided that you (probably) want to make a career in PR and communications. Can you help promote the event, attract wider attention and draw in larger numbers of participants? The answer will almost certainly be 'yes', and – once again – you'll gain valuable experience as well as something interesting and relevant to put on your CV.

Most PR work, most of the time, is about persuading people – in large numbers – to feel, think and do something they wouldn't otherwise have felt, thought or done. It's using the art and science of *persuasive communications* to change people's behaviour.

Is there anything in your local environment – school, neighbourhood, business community, sports or cultural enterprises, college/university, action-groups, cause-related, charitable – anything – where you could volunteer and notch up real-life experience of *persuasive communications*, giving yourself professional knowledge as well as stand-out factors on your CV and employment applications?

WHY THESE EARLY INITIATIVES HELP YOUR CAREER PROSPECTS

We know that PR and communications is a sought-after career. It appeals strongly to people who want to perform creative work in a commercial environment. For this reason, the competition is strong: at the entry-level it's a 'buyer's market'. What this means to you is that *any* relevant experience you can bring to the attention of a future employer will help you stand out from the crowd, and land your first full-time, permanent PR job.

Once you have a few years' professional experience 'under your belt' things change. The competition between employers – agencies and in-house-departments – for experienced PR practitioners is fierce, and you will have more opportunities to do more interesting work, move to a more agreeable environment, earn more money, receive better benefits – but this happens later. Your first challenge is getting your first job in PR.

MINI-PRACTICAL

You are a new member of the team working on PR for Marine Estates, a residential property developer constructing new houses and apartments in coastal towns. Marine wants to build 300 new affordable homes in Sandcliffe, a quiet, old-fashioned sea-port which has no remaining fishing industry but is within commuting distance of the county town, a growing employment hub.

Our stakeholder perceptions audit shows that only 15 per cent of the residents in Sandcliffe welcome the idea of the new homes. They don't like change, they fear the consequences and – because they are older generation – an increase in property values means little to them.

Your team is holding a brainstorm to come up with some ideas.

Using your knowledge of human nature and what you've learnt about people in your own local community, what kind of ideas would you contribute to the brainstorm? Your team complies with the **Brainstorm Rules** – all ideas are good, no debate or argument.

Like them or not, Peter Mandelson and Alastair Campbell were the greatest PR team of the late 20th century – and so far of the 21st. Think of it like this: Tony Blair was 'the product'. Mandelson was the in-house director of corporate affairs. Campbell was the experienced head of the agency brought in to deliver the tactical outcomes of Mandelson's strategy. Both were remorseless and ruthless. One had an intuitive nose for mapping the route the 'PR car' should take. The other was a brilliant driver. Until it all fell apart with the Iraq Dossier. But the lesson there is: never take your own genius for granted.

Christopher Broadbent, Sustainability Consultant
and Co-founder of The Robertsbridge Group

MINI-PRACTICAL

Woden is a Danish company specialising in corporate wi-fi security. They have hired us to manage PR around their first steps in the UK market. Their product, *Loki*, shuts down the possibility of bad actors penetrating a company's information technology security via employees' phones.

Market research shows that large UK companies are well aware of this problem and most have taken steps to protect their systems against it. *Woden* is looking at the small and medium-sized enterprise (SME) sector, where knowledge of the issue is patchy. 50 per cent don't know that the problem exists and the 20 per cent who recognise it don't know that specialist solutions are available.

How can we bring these companies' vulnerability to life in a way that grabs the attention of the media and generates sales enquiries for the *Woden* UK team?

MINI-PRACTICAL

You are interning with a local PR agency before you head off to university. You've taken some initiatives in building your own network of contacts, one of which is joining the city business club. You're at a reception after hearing a visiting speaker and you get talking to a friendly person who turns out to be the marketing director of a well-known local company.

When she finds out that you are working in PR she says: 'That's interesting. I know something about advertising but not much about PR, and I wish I knew more. Tell me – how exactly does PR work?'

What do you say? You need to have your 'elevator pitch' ready for conversations like this – three or four sentences which sum up what PR does in terms that will make the other person want to hear more.

Who Are Stakeholders?

Many years ago the general belief was that PR people existed to manage the media, and that was usually their principal or sole function. The PR department was often called 'the press office'. Time has moved on, and nowadays – although the media's still a vitally important element in nearly all PR work – PR professionals pay close attention to understanding and communicating with all the audiences that matter to their company or client, using 30 or more different channels to do so – one of which is the media.

Stakeholders can be defined as groups of people, or individuals, who can have an effect on the success of the company/client/organisation or who can be affected by the client/company/organisation, or both. Stakeholders can be active – they know they are involved, and are doing something about it – or passive – they are aware, but not doing much – or latent, which means they don't yet know they are stakeholders, but probably will at some point in the future.

Most PR and communications programmes start with a comprehensive stakeholder analysis, often based on a stakeholder perceptions audit and using some kind of prioritisation technique like an Influence/Interest Grid. This is a benchmarking or mapping exercise. Only then can PR people start thinking about the messages they want to project to each stakeholder category and the best ways of putting those messages across.

Once you undertake a stakeholder mapping project, you realise how many different kinds of stakeholder must be taken into account and engaged with – dozens, sometimes hundreds of different groups and individuals, all with their own feelings, opinions, susceptibilities and circumstances. PR people need to know this information in fine detail, otherwise their messages will fail to gain traction.

Stakeholder identification and mapping is one of the most intriguing areas in the practice of PR and communications, a blend of science, research, analysis and insight into human nature. It's also one of the fields where new PR recruits can expect to be involved very early on in their careers.

10

BECOMING A SPECIALIST –
OR NOT

Public relations people are very similar to journalists – most reporters start out as generalists and then, as their careers progress, evolve into experts in specific industries, areas or sectors. But not always. Some journalists prefer to turn their hands to anything, ending up as general news-desk reporters or perhaps as columnists – the famous names at our top media, writing mostly personal opinion pieces about anything that catches their eye.

PR people follow a parallel career path.

If you are at school or university and you think that PR could be the right career for you, the key question right now is: do you want to practice PR and communications *on behalf of an industry, product or cause*, or do you feel that you'd like to make your career in PR, almost regardless of the product, brand, company or cause that you are asked to promote.

If you are *already* strongly attracted to a particular industry or field of human activity, and you feel that PR and communications could be the best use of your talents, it makes sense to start developing PR and communications experience in that industry *right now*. This could mean volunteering, shadowing or working as an intern on a temporary basis. It means saturating yourself in the media covering that industry, joining a relevant trade association or business group ... being a sponge.

Then, whether you do a degree or an apprenticeship – or neither – you will have a *personal career strategy*. You will know which companies or agencies (or charities) you want to work for. As we've said before, this is your starting-point: you can switch later – this is easy in PR and communications – and many people do exactly that.

But if you *don't* have a favourite industry, sector or field ... it's not a problem. This means you think you have the basic PR aptitudes (writing ability, curiosity, good interpersonal skills and so on) but you're not yet sure if you'd like to devote your career to Aviation ... or Zoology ... or anything in between. Your *personal career strategy* should focus on acquiring and developing PR skills, and that means an agency or consultancy is probably the best place for you to start work.

It's often said that you shouldn't bring your personal interests to work ... it's best to keep a dividing line between what you do for a living and what you do for love. That may be true in most professions, but not in PR. *Persuasive communication* means enthusiasm, even passion, because it works better. If you love fashion and want to be in and around fashion 24 hours a day, you will probably be a very effective communicator for a fashion brand.

You might ask: 'If I'm *not* mad about a particular industry, how will I be able to act as a *persuasive communicator* for an employer or client in that sector?'

It might sound strange ... but once you've got the brief from a client, met the people, started learning about the company and the product, begun studying the competition, got familiar with the media who cover that industry ... you *automatically* begin to be very interested in that industry and how to help your client succeed.

I'm not a psychologist, so I can't explain it. Maybe it's like a striker transferring from City to Arsenal – within hours their loyalty has switched to a club that, until last month, they cared nothing about. Anyway, it happens in PR when you start work for a new client – every time.

In an agency you will work across a lot of industries and audiences. You'll be presented with a new client in an industry you don't have much knowledge of but absolutely love working with. You never know where your passion(s) may lie.

Chloe Baker, Strategy Director at Liquid, an integrated
communications consultancy

PR is very rewarding on a personal level. You learn so much about strategy and planning ... how to analyse why things succeeded or why they didn't ... you see the effect of your ideas in the real world – you literally see the results of your work 'out there' – very quickly.

Ben Steele, Communications Officer at Sightsavers

Working in an agency environment exposes you to a wide variety of clients, industries, journalists and colleagues with different skill-sets. This can progress your career and knowl-edge very quickly.

Virginia Hawkins, PR Consultant at Screaming Frog

It helps if you have a strong interest in some commercial area. But, if not, don't worry about the exact nature of your PR career – take time to get some real-world experience ... travel, meet different people ... discover what you like and don't like.

Richard Bailey is an editor, PR educator and former
university lecturer

The variety, the different types of projects and sectors you work in, the interesting people you meet, the freedom and creativity, the appreciation you can receive for your skills ... seeing a direct impact on the public audiences your work is aimed at ... this is very rewarding.

Luke Blair, Director of Communications at an NHS
hospital group

> PR is a very broad church. If you feel PR could be for you, start by thinking about what you'd like to do and who you'd like to do it for. Go online and explore the different parts of the industry. Which appeals most to you? Internal communications? Public affairs? Media relations? Digital? Next think about which sector or industry you'd like to work in.
>
> *Stuart McBride is head of PR for a financial*
> *trade association*

ISSUES AND CRISIS COMMUNICATIONS

This is not *exactly* a specialist area of the PR industry but it is nevertheless regarded by most clients and agencies as a domain requiring specialist expertise. This is partly because there is so much at stake and partly because the way the media and other stakeholders treat a company or brand in serious trouble can be (until you're used to it) a little disconcerting.

Why is so much at stake? Because nearly every factor that matters to a company or an organisation these days depends on *credibility*. This is fragile: once lost, it can take forever to regain, and in some cases never is. As Warren Buffett, the world's most successful investor, was the first to say: a reputation takes years to build and can vanish overnight.

Issues are trends or themes which could have an adverse effect on our client's interests, so they need careful watching. This 'radar' function is extremely interesting and is an area of issues and crisis management where comparatively inexperienced people can make a contribution. Crisis communications management is all about doing and saying the right thing when a big problem strikes out of the blue; a crisis is *by definition* a surprise. As you can imagine, the art of crisis communications is being able to react quickly and creditably when taken by surprise – in other words, being *crisis-ready*.

Crises are the media's favourite stories, so your client can expect to be 'on the front page'. This intense media spotlight is what makes a badly managed crisis *so* damaging: everyone is paying extra attention to the company, brand, charity (or whatever), so what they say and do gets noticed and talked about. If they say and do the right thing, the crisis will probably go away in due course. If not, it could be *very* expensive (BP's Deepwater Horizon disaster and VW's 'cheat-device' saga) and often means curtains for the CEO. In rare cases, the damage is self-inflicted. The phrase 'doing a Ratner' has entered business language.

Whether it's at a corporate or brand level and whether it's business-to-consumer, business-to-business, healthcare, financial services, tech or any other sector, all PR plans need an issues and crisis communications section. Every entity where trust, confidence and credibility matter – which means everything that isn't a monopoly – recognises the importance of being ready to react in a professional and human manner when something disastrous happens.

Several of our expert contributors have mentioned that PR is a field where you can work alongside very senior people at a very young age. Crisis communications is a case in point: the CEO or chair is usually the focus of media interest, so she or he needs close, minute-by-minute support from communications specialists like us.

If you are interested to know more about crisis communications, we recommend an excellent book by Kate Hartley – a highly experienced expert – called Communicate in a Crisis. *It gives specially valuable advice on how to handle the time-sensitive problems caused by a crisis arising on digital and social media.*

MINI-PRACTICAL

We have arranged for a 1,200-word case study about one of our client's customers to be published in a leading trade title. The client is very pleased. Then he rings up, not so pleased. 'I've just had Global Logistics on the phone trying to sell me advertising space!'

This can be difficult. The client retains our agency because he thinks PR is far more productive than advertising and also much more cost-effective. He's right. At the same time, media like Global Logistics cannot survive on thin air: they need advertising support to stay in business.

As the saying goes: 'no media, no PR'.

How can we resolve this dilemma? If our client dislikes the idea of advertising, is there another way his company could help Global Logistics stay afloat? Could they sponsor one of Global Logistics' conferences, or maybe one of the categories in the Global Logistics Annual Awards? Is advertorial a possible alternative?

What would you suggest?

11

INDIVIDUALS AND TEAM PLAYERS

Reporters and journalists – our *media customers* – are, by nature, solo performers. They usually work alone and they like doing so. They are 'outsiders' – not *part* of politics, business, entertainment, sport or whatever other subject they're covering – but, instead, observing from the outside, making judgements, forming opinions and then writing or broadcasting what they think.

Public relations people are the exact opposite. We are team players by nature. Almost everything we do is a co-operative effort. We work in teams to look after our clients (if we work in an agency) and we work in teams to come up with ideas, make plans and present our recommendations to senior people (whether we are working in an agency or in an in-house department). If we draft a piece of copy, a script or a concept on our own (which we usually do), we almost always ask our colleagues to comment, add, adapt or see how they can improve the initial draft.

When you look at a newsroom, what you see is a large number of people all working more-or-less on their own, with minimal contact or collaboration. When you look at a PR office, what you see is the same number of people, but they're constantly talking to each other, enlisting each other's help, asking for other people's specialist knowledge or contacts, checking their own ideas against other people's opinions, brainstorming, chatting, debating, arguing, etc. PR is all about teamwork.

Journalists spend a lot of time in each other's company after work, of course. They are as social as everyone else. It's just that the way media work is structured is, for the most part, solitary – whereas the working environment for most PR people, most of the time, is teams.

Do you know if you are a team player by nature? Or do you prefer to do things on your own?

PR and communications is a more diverse and heterogeneous field than almost any other. It is, as Stuart McBride says, 'a broad church'. Even so, it is more likely to appeal to people who are *team players* than to those who see themselves as *lone wolves*.

There are several reasons why this is the case. One is that great communications ideas only occasionally emerge from a single person's mind, and more often from the blending of several different people's experiences and outlooks. Then there is the role played by 'esprit de corps' in generating the enthusiasm which impels much of the proactive, experimental and original thinking that lies behind exceptional PR and communications.

We could cite the need to understand and take a keen interest in how other people feel, think and behave. This is fundamental to successful PR and communications work, and it's more likely to be a characteristic of team players – those who enjoy being and working in the company of others – than in the more isolated preferences of a 'solo artiste'. Whatever the reason, you'll be a natural for PR if you are a team player and you'll find fewer opportunities, and probably less career satisfaction, if you're not.

HOW TO TELL IF YOU'RE A NATURAL TEAM PLAYER

Do you need to be the star of the show? Do other people consider that you have an extra-strong ego? This is not a defect – far from it – but it's a clue that PR might not be the ideal career choice for you.

Employers want team players and look for signs that interviewees might not be naturally suited to the collaborative, co-operative world of successful PR teams. They watch for people who say 'I' more than 'we' when describing successes. They look for a readiness to criticise other colleagues – a Red Flag.

Do you get a buzz out of helping other people be successful? Are you as happy to make an assist as to score a goal? Or *more* happy? Do you get more personal pleasure out of the success of your team than from accolades for your personal contribution? You don't need to be a shrinking violet – it's about the thrill of being part of a successful group.

Do you consider yourself to be an *empathetic* person? As our contributors have said, empathy is the source of fellow-feeling and, therefore, of the ability to address audiences in language which means something to them. It's also the wellspring of being a team player.

Do you celebrate the success of your team-mates, personally and publicly? It's fine to be competitive – of course – but it's better in a PR team to be the kind of person who helps colleagues do well and feels great about making a contribution to the team's success.

> *My game-plan was simple. I only hired people who were cleverer, sharper, smarter, more knowledgeable, more talented and generally better than me. The more successful they were, the more money I made. (Quote from anonymous founder of Top 50 UK PR agency)*

How do you resolve disagreements and differences of opinion? Do you need to come out on top? One of our clients, a large electronics company, had a 'golden rule' for negotiations: they were only considered successful if both sides felt they had won.

The distinction between individualists and team players can be fuzzy. A first chair violinist is part of an orchestra … Bill Gates relied on Paul Allen … Harry Kane needs other people to enable him to work his magic … Max Verstappen has 1,200 people behind him … the Saatchi brothers had hundreds of experts working in the agency that made them famous … your favourite stand-up depends on the jokes written by anonymous geniuses in the background…

There *are* stars in PR. But not many. Most super-successful PR created spaces (companies, agencies, frameworks and structures) for other PR people to achieve personal success by working in teams.

Which are you? If you think you're a team player – or you already know you are – PR and communications could be a natural and fulfilling career for you. If you feel happier working on your own, PR isn't excluded – there are plenty of PR planners and analysts who work more-or-less alone – *but* you might find that a different line of work would suit you better.

MINI-PRACTICAL

Here is an ethical problem. We are the PR department of a housebuilding company which has enjoyed steadily growing sales and profits over the last eight years. But last year was a bit of a disaster: sales fell by 20 per cent and profits were all but wiped out. This has never happened before and the chief executive officer (CEO) is worried that the company's reputation with customers, investors and planning authorities will take a serious hit.

We have an interview coming up with a leading trade title, which has always given our company positive coverage. The journalist will ask about the annual figures, as usual. The CEO thinks the best plan is to give her false numbers showing no growth but no decline year-on-year. We know that this is not only a very bad idea but also contravenes our professional Code of Conduct.

How can we persuade the CEO to face the music and tell the truth?

12

HOW TO DEVELOP YOUR PR
AND COMMUNICATIONS SKILLS

You are considering public relations and communications as a career choice. Or you may *already* be certain that this is the profession that you want to enter. There are certain skills you can set out to acquire and improve, *at any age*, which will help you land the PR job you want and also help you do well once you start working in a PR agency or department.

It's worth pointing out right up-front that these skills *are* specific to PR and communications but *not* exclusive to PR – they will be valuable in whatever career you eventually decide to pursue. We hope you will choose PR ... but, as you know, although PR is right for a very wide variety of people, it's not right for everyone.

Here are the key skills and how to improve your mastery of them.

Reading with an analytical, critical point of view. Most PR work involves looking at text or hearing verbal briefings provided by other people – clients, marketing people, the C-Suite, the boss – and trying to figure out how to translate what they say into short, sharp, cogent content which will catch the interest of audiences, encourage them to read on and ultimately change their knowledge, feelings, perceptions, ideas and behaviour.

This is the hardest thing in the world.

It starts with picking out what really matters from the verbiage. This is a kind of forensic skill that – if you've done a university course – is probably how you set about constructing essays.

Either way, you need to develop a *sceptical* frame of mind – like a journalist – to sort the wheat from the chaff.

How can you develop your ability to marshal the facts that matter and discard the rest? Make a habit of looking at media material and pulling it apart (mentally). Look at other sources to see how *they* have portrayed the same story. Spot the differences in angle, slant, their use of sources and talking heads, the way real facts and figures are used – or not.

This is a different kind of reading (or listening, viewing, browsing). You are sharpening your ability to take a brief and think about it in a way that *could* result in a credible editorial.

Writing short, concise copy that 'feeds the mind and touches the heart'. How to improve? Write a lot – either for publication or simply for your own purposes. Spend at least two hours a day writing. When you work in PR and communications, it will be more like three or four.

Read the best media writing and try to see how those authors achieve their effects. Imitate their techniques in your own writing. It's a cliche that the best way to improve your writing is to read what good writers have written, but it's true.

Oddly, some of the best English media writing can be found in the United States.

In this country, we have the *Guardian*, which regularly wins awards for composition and design. I recommend their long-form pieces – models of really good, well-researched media writing.

We also have the *FT* (accuracy, accuracy, accuracy ... but a little colourless) and the *Economist* (brainy but opinionated). Then we have periodicals like the *TLS*, *New Statesman* and *Spectator* which pride themselves on the quality of their journalism ... you decide.

In the United States, we have the *New York Times* (in a class of its own for well-researched, fact-checked and well-written journalism) and current affairs magazines which spend a lot of money on the quality of their content and contributors – *Atlantic* and *New Yorker*. The United States also offers the world's best business journalism: *Fortune*, *Forbes*, *Bloomberg Businessweek* and a host of online titles covering specialist areas.

Speaking to audiences large and small is part of a successful PR person's professional skill set. You will probably be addressing audiences yourself, and even when you're not you will be writing scripts and presentations for your clients or spokespeople. When you work in a PR agency or department, you will receive presentation training.

Before then, I recommend you spend hours watching famous speakers and presenters on YouTube. What are they doing to achieve their effects? What methods have they mastered? Public speaking is a *performance art* with rules and techniques. Most people need to learn how to do it well. One short cut is to join a local or university dramatic group.

Storytelling is simpler than it sounds. It just means catching and keeping the attention of an audience. Avoid giving long lists of facts and figures … avoid legal or corporate language … instead, turn your content into a *personal narrative* delivered in quotes or as reported speech by your spokesperson. Plain, everyday vocabulary. Vivid and lively (especially in business-to-business media writing, where this is rare). Frame your narrative as what happened to the speaker or writer, how they felt about it, what they said or did next. We *all* prefer stories to statements.

Thinking in pictures can be tricky when all our school or college work has been word-based, but psychologists recommend it as a good way to free up our imaginative powers. Einstein said he never thought in words, but in images and symbols which he then combined. There are lots of techniques online for thinking in diagrams, in the round, getting away from lists and linearity. You may already think mainly in pictures, but, if not, it's a good plan to develop this facility – it will be super-useful in your PR and communications career.

Psychology is at the heart of successful persuasive communication. You may be lucky enough to possess good insight into human nature – perhaps you are naturally intuitive. But if you're like the rest of us, time spent reading and learning about psychology is never wasted. We've mentioned *Behavioural Economics*, and that's a good place to start. The best way to find out about Behavioural

Economics is to watch Rory Sutherland's talks, presentations and interviews on YouTube. Then there's a whole shelf of great books about it if you want to explore further.

Digital and social ... you already know how important internet-based channels are for disseminating news and shaping public opinion. You know how fast this sector changes. It can be an effort to keep up, but all we can say here is that the effort is worth making for professional purposes: whether you use particular platforms or not, you'll need to know which ones will work for your clients or employers. The most effective options in two years' time might not even exist yet.

Finally, spend as much time in the company of media and PR people as you can. There are associations and clubs you can join, all around the country. Go along and listen to what they're talking about. Get an idea of the kind of people they are (varied, of course, but with certain characteristics in common). Do you feel at home? Are these the kind of people you want to work alongside in your professional career? If the answer's yes, listening to them will teach you more about PR and communications than any book can.

If you like books, there are two which we recommend for your attention. Robert Cialdini's Influence: The Psychology of Persuasion *is full of surprising facts and, because he's a witty author, a pleasure to read. The best book on the market if you want a factual, comprehensive portrait of the PR industry is* PR Today *by Trevor Morris.*

MINI-PRACTICAL

We are working for a highly successful online fashion retailer. It's an ultra-competitive industry, all about low prices and the rapid introduction of new styles. Our client has developed a super-efficient logistics operation; customers like their ability to fulfil orders within an average of two days – anywhere in the United Kingdom. Thanks to our work, the CEO has become something of a guru in the world of fast fashion. The company's investors are planning an IPO within a year.

Then ... disaster. The International Consortium of Investigative Journalists has revealed that some of our client's products are manufactured in sweatshops in the Philippines. They've got footage of workers who seem to be as young as 12 operating sewing-machines in a ramshackle shed ... and the tops being made are recognisably one of our client's biggest sellers.

We are called at 10 p.m. to a crisis meeting with the CEO and the marketing director. We need to think quickly: what can the CEO say and do to quell the storm which is starting to spiral on social media?

Longer-term, what can our client do to regain the confidence and respect of their other stakeholders – including investors, trading standards and the heavyweight media?

13

WILL YOU BE RICH?
THE FINANCIAL SIDE

Probably not! If making money is your goal, you'd do better in the city, in a law firm or in management consultancy. But if you have a vocation for investment management, the law or corporate re-structuring, you're unlikely to be considering a career in communications.

Public relations is one of the *creative industries*, which means PR and communications people use their imagination and creativity at work every single day. If this sounds like an attractive career for you, earning serious money is probably not your number one priority.

Most PR people make a good living, some of them make a very good living and *some* make a great deal of money.

They say that work can make you rich, happy or famous. All the PR people I have ever known – with very few exceptions – enjoy what they do and look forward to starting work every morning. Remuneration is important (of course) but it's rarely their main concern.

WHAT YOU CAN EXPECT TO EARN

The average starting salary in PR (in 2025) is around £20,000. You can expect to be promoted every two or three years (or even faster) so, in your late twenties, you will earn £30,000 to £40,000 as an account manager. After that, it's all a question of talent, ambition and opportunity. Senior account people earn anywhere from £60,000 to £100,000 and associates or board directors anywhere between £100,000 and £200,000.

Specialist areas like public affairs, financial communications or healthcare tend to pay more; popular areas like fashion, the arts or entertainment tend to pay somewhat less.

DOES *ANYONE* GET RICH IN PR?

Yes. If you have entrepreneurial flair as well as PR skills, you could be one of the 30 or 40 people every year who set up their own PR agencies or consultancies. These are usually (but not always) specialists in one area or another, normally based on the knowledge, interests and experience of their founders.

PR agency start-ups are usually partnerships rather than the property of single individuals. If they grow and are well-run, their owners receive shareholders' dividends as well as a salary for their day-to-day work. PR agency earnings in the United Kingdom range from 10 to 20 per cent (on average) so a small-to-medium-sized agency with revenues of £2 million can produce substantial annual returns for the people who own it.

As the agency grows, the owners will typically invite other senior people to join them as shareholders. You can therefore enjoy the benefits of agency ownership without necessarily leaving to set up a new firm.

Successful agencies usually receive approaches after a few years from larger companies who want to acquire them. This is the point at which the founders and other shareholders can make a considerable amount of money. Acquirers typically pay a price between 5 and 10 times annual earnings, so a firm with £5 million revenues and 20 per cent earnings will deliver somewhere between £5m and £10m to its owners, usually in staged payments or 'tranches' over (usually) three years.

These kinds of payments can, of course, be life-changing – but only a small number of the new agencies started every year succeed in achieving the consistent growth that attracts the attention of an acquirer.

WHAT KIND OF BENEFITS ARE AVAILABLE?

'A PR agency is only as good as the people who work for it.' Clients say this and agency owners know it, so they make every effort to ensure that their employees are happy in their work, feel appreciated, sense they are making progress, and remain loyal as long as possible.

You can expect to receive a number of *benefits* as a result. (If not ... hmm). First on the list would be training and continuing professional development (CPD). Up-to-date professional skills and knowledge are what clients look for, so employers invest in providing their people with as much training, coaching and skills-enhancement as they can afford. This is typically provided in-house by colleagues and is often combined with training sessions run by, for example, the PRCA.

Next would be financial benefits of one kind or another. Some agencies provide loans to enable commuter staff to buy season tickets. Some operate a cycle-to-work scheme. Some provide pension schemes – these can be generous, since young people struggling to pay the rent can rarely make saving for a pension a priority. Some enrol employees in private medical/health insurance schemes. Some pay for membership of professional associations.

Most agencies operate one or more *bonus schemes*: these give employees periodic extra sums based on the whole company's financial performance, or their department's or team's performance. Some companies also give 'spot bonuses' for exceptional individual work.

Then there are benefits like gym-membership, social events hosted by the company after-hours and 'awaydays' – a chance for everyone to get to know each other, do some collaborative work and enjoy the attractions of somewhere like Seville. Or Southampton.

When it comes to entitlements like sick-leave and maternity/paternity, PR agencies are almost always at the top of the tree. Because 'the people are the product' PR agency employees can expect to be well-treated and well-looked-after.

How about in-house PR departments? Here you would expect to receive the normal benefits available to everyone employed by a large company, organisation or institution. These *can*, for obvious reasons, be superior to those available from smaller firms.

RICH, FAMOUS, HAPPY?

If you choose PR and communications as a career, you are unlikely to become famous (though your clients will). You may be one of the few who possess entrepreneurial ability and drive, and one day get rich – but, statistically, that's improbable. However, you will *certainly* earn a good living and you will *definitely* be happy.

If you think PR might be for you: most importantly of all you have to like people. It's not only the most essential asset in PR, it's just as true of politicians. You can't learn this. If you don't know what I'm talking about PR is not for you.

You need to know instinctively when to let the other person talk, even if you might disagree with them. There's just a chance they might be right.

You have to feel comfortable initiating a conversation – perhaps over the phone – with someone who doesn't know you. It's not easy, but – once done – the sense of satisfaction makes it worth the effort.

You have to be able to take occasional rejection – even rudeness – in your stride. Some people will use you as a punchbag – as a substitute for their own inadequacy.

When acting for a client you know from Day One it's the *client* who you are there to help. That might mean advising a client that their pet strategy is wrong, if that's what you believe.

You need to be sensitive enough to know how to give that advice and live with the consequences.

One big tip is that a person who will be a success in PR is someone who looks forward to work rather than dreading it.

Steve Norris is an entrepreneur, author and former Minister of Transport

14

TYPICAL QUESTIONS

Public Relations people seem to be extroverts, very sociable and confident, good at talking. I'm a quieter type of person – not shy, exactly, but not eager to be the centre of attention. Should I be thinking of PR as a career?

Yes, definitely. It's not really true that PR people are loud and talkative. Those are just the ones you notice. Most PR people are better at listening than speaking. They soak up what everyone else is saying, combine it with research data and then compose a plan, a speech, a script or an item of media material. If you like this kind of analytical work and have a flair for writing, you should certainly consider a career in PR and communications.

It's also worth mentioning that a PR career is one of the best ways to find out what your real potential and interests are – because it is so varied, diverse and multidisciplinary. You are encouraged to experiment and you get exposed to challenges much earlier than in many other types of professional business services roles.

I spend a lot of time on social media and get most of my information about what's happening in the world from my favourite platforms. Do I need to read other kinds of media for a career in PR?

The short answer is yes. Social media outlets are important and, of course, engaging, but they are only one part of the array of distribution channels which PR people have to learn about and use.

It's a good idea, if you are thinking of a PR career, to widen your range of media consumption and also to consume media content which is *not* in alignment with your own views and preferences. Employers rate new recruits who are *foxes* (they know something about a lot of things) as well as *hedgehogs* (who know a lot about a single thing).

We hear about 'spin' from time to time. Is PR ethical?

The Codes of Conduct of the Public Relations and Communications Association (PRCA) and the Chartered Institute of Public Relations (CIPR) are clear and rigorous. For example, it is forbidden to knowingly issue a falsehood. Any person or firm found guilty of this offence risks expulsion from their professional body. Both the PRCA and the CIPR require members to sign up to these Codes of Conduct and they maintain investigative committees which step in when they spot likely infractions or when a complaint is received about a member's behaviour.

The Codes of Conduct can be studied on the websites of the PRCA (prca.org.uk) and the CIPR (cipr.co.uk).

I have heard that working in PR can be very stressful. Is this a problem?

It's true that, like most creative and service industries, PR can be high-pressure. But not all the time. PR people mostly work in teams, so they can always get a helping hand when the workload piles up. Employers take great care to see that people are *not* subjected to undue pressure. However, as our contributors have pointed out, PR is unpredictable and no two days are the same. There is no such thing as a steady routine – or, at least, not for long. If you are the kind of person who enjoys the excitement of unexpected challenges, you will be happy with the pace of life in PR. But if you really prefer an orderly kind of career, where you know more or less what will happen tomorrow and next Thursday, the sometimes frenetic nature of PR might not be your cup of tea.

I like the idea of being a professional communicator, but I'm not sure I really want to work in industry and commerce. Are there options?'

Very much so. If you are drawn towards *public service*, you'll find that every government department, every police force, every fire service, every NHS trust, every university, every local authority, every public transport provider (and so on) maintains its own PR and communications team, and sometimes retains specialist outside agencies as well. Most charities, non-profits and philanthropic bodies likewise. The quality of *public* and *third-sector* PR teams is very high – they provide excellent training, they consistently win PR and Communications Awards, and they are sought-after employers.

What if I join a PR team as an intern or first job and don't get on with my manager?

According to the statistics, a good 'boss' is the main reason why people stay with an employer and a bad 'boss' is the main reason they leave – not just in PR but in any job.

If this happens to you, the chances are that your colleagues will be ready to help and advise. In the end, you may need to ask for a 'heart-to-heart' with your manager and tell her how you feel. She might be amazed to hear that you're unhappy.

In organisations with HR departments, there'll be a set procedure for seeking advice from the professional Human Resources specialists, and a system in place.

It sounds as if PR people need to be sensitive but also very resilient. How does that work?

Suppose you've got a client story that you're trying to place with an important outlet. Time and again the journalists say 'Not really for us, thank you'. This happens a lot and it's frustrating. But it's not personal. Suppose you're part of a pitch team ... you've all worked hard and given (you think) a winning performance ... then the call comes: 'You were a close second'. All that work for nothing! It can be depressing.

Nothing is guaranteed in PR. To enjoy it and succeed you need a 'can do' attitude and quite a lot of determination. Maybe more than in most other careers.

Is PR really the same as advertising?

No, though it often shares a similar purpose. The big difference is credibility. PR mainly operates through independent, trustworthy third parties like editorial media. We usually believe what these sources tell us. An advertiser tells us their product is fantastic, and with any luck they'll entertain or amuse us at the same time. But we're never quite sure if we can believe what they say.

Unlike advertising, PR sets out to engage audiences in a *conversation*. PR is interactive, thrives on feedback and constantly fine-tunes its messages and channels accordingly. Advertising, as a rule, is more interested in spectacular, broad-brush, big-budget attempts to dominate the audience's attention.

Advertising and PR used to be thought of as fish and fowl, but nowadays they are more likely to work together than in opposition. Most advertising agencies have a PR brand and most PR firms are happy to create, produce and place advertising.

They are both *creative industries* in the business of *persuasive communications*. But they use different skills and achieve their objectives in different ways.

How do journalists really *feel about PR people?*

Mixed, as you'll find out when you talk to a reporter over a coffee, a pint or a glass of Pinot Grigio. They rely on the PR industry to supply them with the majority of the content, which they process and publish – but they'd prefer not to. However, the days when newsrooms were self-sustaining are long gone. This can be a source of regret for older journalists.

Journalists tend to complain, when given the chance, about the *quality* of most PR. They say that most PR people don't know what news is, don't understand how the media work and can't write.

If you want to win the respect of your media customers as a *fellow-professional*, the key is learning how to write in a way they admire. Journalists spend a long time perfecting their media writing skills. If you offer them copy which complies with their own rules and conventions, you are half-way to earning their good opinion.

I've heard PR described as 'smoke and mirrors'. Can PR results be measured?'

This is another legacy from the old, old days when PR was thought of as a mysterious, dark art. It brings with it the peculiar idea that PR results should be equated with advertising – as if PR was just a different way of obtaining media space and time – hence the fraud of AVEs, or *advertising value equivalents*.

Nowadays PR people and their clients use data analytics to monitor a host of metrics in real time. The most important are *outcomes* (or impact) – did this PR initiative catch the attention of its target audiences, did it make them think, do they remember what was said, have they changed their perceptions, preferences, opinions and behaviour as a result? If so, how? If not, why not? These numbers enable PR people to adjust messages and channels while a campaign or programme is under way, with the objective of improving return on investment.

For more about the science of monitoring PR results, check out the website of the International Association for the Measurement and Evaluation of Communication (amecorg.com)

Can PR work be boring?

It's probably the least boring career you can imagine. But in rare instances, a PR role *can* be frustrating and therefore boring. For example, there are some organisations who really *don't* want to engage with the media, so they employ PR people to keep them at arm's length. This is the exact opposite of what PR professionals are there to do, but it happens.

Or you might have a client who has no spirit of adventure. They are just too timid to step off the well-beaten pathway and do something different from what everybody else is doing. This can make PR people tear their hair out, become despondent or – perhaps – set out on the long road to persuading their client that *being different* is the soul of PR success. But for many, life is too short ... there are better opportunities elsewhere.

There always are. No PR person ever needs to be stuck in a boring role.

The essence of successful PR is creativity, imagination and origi-nality. PR people spend a lot of time just thinking up new ideas. If this sounds like having fun at work ... it is!

PR is demanding, competitive, high-pressure at times, problem-atical, challenging, difficult and unpredictable ... but it offers more sheer enjoyment than any other professional services roles that we know of.

MINI-PRACTICAL

We are facing a difficult ethical problem.

We went out last night for drinks with a group of young traders from our client, an investment bank. Late in the evening one of them started bragging to his colleagues about an insider-trading ploy he'd just pulled off. Most of them laughed but one or two looked distinctly unamused.

We are in a spot. We have heard someone admit illegal behaviour. If what he says is true (we don't know if it is) and it's discovered, both he and his employer – our client – will be hit with severe penalties.

Should we pretend we heard nothing, and leave it to his colleagues to report him to the bank? We can't really do that if we take our professional Code of Conduct seriously. At the same time, we don't want to wreck his career if – as seems possible – he was just trying to get attention after too many drinks.

We might decide that we're too junior to make a decision like this (very true) and 'delegate upwards' by informing our account director. But even this would set in train a series of events which could have drastic consequences for the young trader and our client.

What would you do?

We Are the Drill!

'*People don't want a quarter-inch drill. What they want is a quarter-inch hole.*'

This is worth remembering when you're in PR. We enjoy our work so much that we can sometimes lose sight of why we're being paid. As one of our clients said: 'You people seem to have set up a sports and social club which somehow finances itself! Be careful you don't end up living in a PR bubble'.

No client or employer wants PR per se. They see PR and communications as a means to an end – usually expressed in financial or other numbers: higher sales, a better margin, a stronger share-price, higher-quality recruits, a larger market-share and so on. They pay us because they believe our skills will help them achieve their numerical targets – more quickly and at lower cost.

As you can tell from our contributors' comments, most people in PR love it. But never forget: we are the drill.

APPENDIX 1: SOURCES OF FURTHER INFORMATION

Industry bodies providing news, advice, research, opinion, blogs, essays and a variety of helpful services for people wanting to know more about public relations and communications:

The Public Relations and Communications Association (prca.org.uk).
The Chartered Institute of Public Relations (cipr.co.uk).
The International Public Relations Association (ipra.org).
The Institute for Public Relations (instituteforpr.org).
The International Association for the Measurement and Evaluation of Communication (amecorg.com).

Specialist media providing news and commentary about PR:

PR Week (prweek.com).
Communicate Magazine (communicatemagazine.com).
PRovoke Media (provokemedia.com).

University careers services:
Many university careers services offer guidance on careers in PR and communications. Check out your own university's site, then see what other universities have to say.

Recruitment/employment agencies:
Recruitment specialists like Reed, Indeed, Taylor Birchwood and Reuben Sinclair offer a wealth of useful information and advice on their websites. The Taylor Bennett Foundation offers six professional development programmes for young people from ethnic minority backgrounds who are interested in a career in PR and communications.

PR agency/consultancy websites:
Most sites not only give a portrait of their agency but also provide think pieces, research, blogs and case studies which will fill out your picture of the industry as a whole. A good place to start would be the Public Relations and Communications Association's membership list.

APPENDIX 2: PUBLIC RELATIONS AND COMMUNICATIONS TERMINOLOGY

Advertising: Space or time paid for by the advertiser, and known to be.

Advertising value equivalent (AVEs): Discredited way of calculating editorial return on investment (ROI).

Advertorial: Media material which resembles editorial but is actually paid for by an advertiser.

Agency: Specialist firm acting on behalf of clients. Also known as consultancy.

Angle, slant: Reporter's point of view in a story. Can be broadly positive (up), negative (down) or neutral.

Astroturfing: Making a product, company, cause or party *appear* to have popular support.

Audience analysis: Research giving quantitative and qualitative data about target audience perceptions.

B-roll: Corporate or brand footage supplied to broadcasters to illustrate news items.

Behavioural economics (BE): Combination of economics with psychology, sociology, neuroscience and research.

Block-and-bridge: Media training technique used to avoid answering tricky interview questions.

Boilerplate: Standard information, often added at the end of a media release or advisory.

Brand: Distinctive name, look, logo, sound or symbol aiding product memorability.

Brand character analysis: Forensic examination of a brand or product.

Brand loyalty: Emotional attachment to a specific brand name. Brand-owner's nirvana.

Briefing: Formal sharing of information ... client to agency, agency to media.

Business-to-consumer (B2C): The primary audience is people in their private capacity.

Business-to-business (B2B): Public relations aimed at people acting in a professional capacity.

Byline: Journalist's name under headline. Valued by people in the media.

Case study: Feature describing how a product or service has been used successfully by a customer.

Channels, platforms: Options for communicating with audiences – mainly used to describe social media.

Chartered Institute of Public Relations (CIPR): One of two UK professional bodies.

Community relations: When a company sets out to engage closely with its local neighbours.

Content: Anything written for publication – also known as *stories* and *material*.

Copywriting: The art of writing for publication, either advertising or PR.

Copy taster: A sub-editor who filters incoming stories for editorial consideration.

Corporate communications: Managing interaction and engagement with *all* a company's stakeholders.

Corporate social responsibility/investment (CSR/CSI): When companies want to demonstrate good corporate citizenship.

Coverage: Publication of PR material in independent media outlets.

Crisis communications: Managing PR in a crisis to minimise or neutralise reputational damage.

Deadline: Time when items *must* be ready for publication or broadcast (very strict in the media).

Embargo: Item issued in advance but not for publication before a specified date/time.

Event management: Conferences, seminars, round-tables, open-houses, etc – a large part of a PR person's work.

Exclusive: Story given to a single journalist. Highly prized by the media. Used to be 'scoop'.

Facility visit: Look-see opportunity for media to a plant, location, laboratory, site, etc.

Financial communications: Specialist practice serving banking, insurance etc. Includes investor relations.

Freelancer: Self-employed journalist, usually trade, technical and professional media (TTP) specialist, often an ex-staffer.

Government relations: Specialist practice trying to influence legislators and regulators.

Grassroots campaign: Generating genuine popular support for a company, cause, etc. (cf. 'astroturfing').

Infographics: Presentation of data in illustrated form. Valuable PR or specialist skill.

Influencer: Digital/social figure with a large following, prepared to promote products/services.

In-house: A PR and communications team employed by a company or organisation.

Internal communications: Engaging and communicating with employees. Can be part of public relations and/or human resources.

Investor relations: Specialist practice communicating with actual and potential shareholders.

Issues monitoring and management: Scanning for potential PR problems before they become problems.

Key decision maker (KDM): People who make the ultimate decisions in corporate or political contexts.

Key opinion former (KOF): People whose advice helps KDMs arrive at their decisions.

Key performance indicators (KPIs). How clients judge agencies' effectiveness.

Lobbying: The art of presenting a convincing case to a political KDM or KOF.

Mainstream media (MSM): Branded titles, originally newspapers and magazines plus TV/radio. Trusted sources.

Media advisory: Alerts media to an upcoming event which (we hope) will interest them.

Media monitoring: Collecting, analysing and reporting on coverage for impact, tone, accuracy and so on.

Media relations: The art of establishing mutually beneficial connections with editors and journalists.

Message: The commercial 'call to action' embedded in effective media material.

Newswire: Supply services for 'hard' news often owned by media consortia.

Op-ed: News-feature giving someone's opinion. Can carry client's byline.

Off the record: Spoken media information for background, not publication.

Outcomes: The measured, numerical consequences of a PR initiative.

Outlet: Omnibus term covering all channels, publications, titles, stations, programmes, etc.

Paid, Earned, Shared, Owned (PESO) model: Communications Venn diagram invented by Gini Dietrich.

Pitch: How clients choose agencies; also how agencies try to place stories with journalists.

Press kit, press pack: Information dossier for journalists. Once physical, now mostly digital.

Press release: Basic instrument of most PR work with the media.

Product placement: Getting a client's product visible in movies and shows. Usually paid-for.

Public affairs: The general practice area of government relations and lobbying.

Public relations: The art and science of managing reputation, perceptions, prominence and popularity.

Public Relations and Communications Association (PRCA): One of two UK professional bodies.

Publicity: Catch-all term for advertising, marketing communications and PR.

Q&A: Document preparing spokespeople for interviews with media and stakeholders.

Reputation management: Taking responsibility for the totality of a company's stakeholder interactions.

ROI: Method of assessing effectiveness of money spent on PR and communications.

Search engine optimisation (SEO): Technical practice of achieving better prominence in online exposure.

Share-of-voice: Prominence versus competitors, established by media monitoring.

Spokesperson: Designated 'face and voice' of a company or brand. Often chief executive officer or chair.

Sponsorship: Paid-for association of brands with sports, celebrities, cultural events, etc.

Stakeholder: Anyone who's affected by, or could affect, a company or organisation.

Sub: Media employees who specialise in improving journalists' copy.

Trade, Technical and Professional (TTP) media: target for most B2B PR.

Unique Selling Proposition (USP): The single attribute that makes a product or brand different and better.

White paper: Think piece setting out an organisation's expert view. Often a forecast.

ABOUT THE AUTHOR

Adrian Wheeler, MA FCIPR FPRCA, has worked all his life as a Public Relations Consultant in the United Kingdom, Europe, the United States and the Gulf. He is the author of *Crisis Communications Management* and *Writing for the Media,* both published by Emerald Worldwide. He is a recipient of the Sir Stephen Tallents Medal for services to the PR industry.